COOKIES, COOKIES & more COOKIES!

An Imagine Book
Published by Charlesbridge
85 Main Street, Watertown, MA 02472
617-926-0329
www.charlesbridge.com

Created by Penn Publishing Ltd.
1 Yehuda Halevi Street, Tel Aviv, Israel 65135
www.penn.co.il

Design and layout by Michal & Dekel
Editing and food styling by Deanna Linder
Photography by Danya Weiner

Library of Congress Cataloging-in-Publication Data

German, Lilach.
Cookies, cookies & more cookies! / Lilach German;
photography by Danya Weiner.
p. cm.
ISBN 978-1-936140-23-7 (reinforced for library use)
1. Cookies. 2. Cookbooks. I. Weiner, Danya. II. Title.
III. Title: Cookies, cookies and more cookies!
TX772.G43 2011
641.8'654--dc22
2010038692

2 4 6 8 10 9 7 5 3 1

Printed in China
Manufactured in December, 2010

For information about custom editions, special sales,
premium and corporate purchases, please contact
Charlesbridge Publishing at specialsales@charlesbridge.com

COOKIES, COOKIES & more COOKIES!

Lilach German

PHOTOGRAPHY BY

DANYA WEINER

imagine!
Publishing

Contents

Introduction

Some believe that the first cookie was actually a "test" for a cake recipe. According to this theory, the baker used a small amount of ingredients to test the successfulness of the recipe, the oven temperature and the combination of tastes. Mixing the small amount of ingredients worked! The earliest known American cookbooks support this theory; cookies were always listed under a subcategory in the cakes section, and never stood alone. Furthermore, the origin of the word "cookie" derives from the Dutch word *koekje*, which means "small cake". It is believed that cookies originated in the 7th century AD in Persia, where the use of sugar was particularly common. Local Persian bakers would sell their merchandise to wealthy members of royalty.

During the Age of Exploration, cookies became an ideal treat due to their especially long shelf-life and their sweet and nourishing character, leading to the spread of cookie recipes throughout many different regions. Today, countless cookie recipes exist. They come from numerous origins, with each country maintaining its own characteristic cookies. The fact that cookies are easy to make, generally consist of readily available ingredients, and of course, have a great taste, have made these baked goods extremely popular over a long span of time. Today, new cookie recipes are being developed in the most modern and advanced kitchens, and the classic, well-known recipes are still favored among the masses.

The smell of freshly baked cookies automatically takes me back to the days of childhood, visiting my grandmother on the weekends, both of us cutting cookies out of homemade cookie dough. My grandmother would always give me a little piece of the dough to play with, and I would make the dough into cookies of abstract shapes of my liking. I clearly

remember impatiently waiting for the cookies to finish baking, and when they were ready, we would sprinkle on mounds of powdered sugar, and I would eat them while they were still soft and warm.

The wonderful thing about baking cookies is that they are so simple to make; even those who don't consider themselves a whiz in the kitchen can enjoy making homemade, beautifully tasting cookies. Their simplicity and relatively short preparation time makes cookies a great treat to make with children, providing them with the sweet, creative experience of making something handmade. I hope that you enjoy baking these cookies for your family and friends, and delight in eating them even more!

About the Author

Lilach German is the founder of Lilach Food and Design, a successful gourmet catering company. Lilach studied at the prestigious Le Cordon Bleu School in Paris and is the author of the book "Cupcakes, Cupcakes & More Cupcakes!".

Tools

*Most of the tools used in these recipes
are basic and can be found
in every home kitchen.
The more professional tools
used in a few recipes, such as
a baking thermometer and digital scale, are
great to have for all your baking needs
and are worth the investment.*

Cookie Cutters

Cookie cutters can be found in home-goods and craft stores. Generally made of metal or plastic, they come in every shape and size imaginable. They should be washed and dried after every use, due to their tendency to rust. In general, most cookie cutters have a smooth, rounded side and shaper side, which should be used facing downwards, for cutting dough. If you start to make a cookie recipe and have forgotten your cutters, be creative and use what you have in the kitchen, such as a cup (used upside down). Even when a specific cookie cutter is listed in a recipe, you may use a different cutter of your choice. Just keep in mind that the yield will differ to what is listed.

Fine Sieve/Sifter

You can use a professional baking sifter, but a small colander made of fine-mesh wire will work just as well. The purpose of sifting is to aerate flour, which makes it light and fluffy, therefore giving the same effect to the finished product. This step should not be omitted. Ingredients should be measured or weighed after being sifted.

Measuring Tools

Baking is an exact science and it is important to stick to the amounts listed in the recipes. Therefore, I highly suggest working with measuring devices, such as a digital scale, measuring cups, measuring spoons, professional baking thermometer, etc. Measuring tools can be bought at nearly all home goods stores.

Mixer

All of the recipes in this book can be made using your hands to mix. Although it is sometimes more enjoyable to work dough with your hands, an electric mixer expedites the preparation work and also allows for a more sterile and clean environment. Each recipe details the mixer attachment needed, either whisk or paddle. It is very important not to overwork the dough. While mixing, you should stop the mixer every so often and scrape down the sides using a flexible spatula to make sure that all ingredients are evenly incorporated. I like to let the mixer do three quarters of the work and then I finish kneading with my hands, until I reach the desired consistency

Oven

Ovens range greatly in functionality and strength; therefore it is important to keep in mind that the given baking times should be considered in relation to your particular oven. You should bake cookies on the middle rack of the oven, rotating halfway through, allowing them to bake as evenly as possible. In addition, if the cookies come out soft after the given baking time, don't be alarmed—cookies harden once they reach room temperature.

Pastry Bags & Decorating Tips

Also known as piping bags, pastry bags can be purchased at specialty cooking shops, along with an assortment of matching tips. Decorating tips come in various sizes and shapes, allowing for a vast choice of designs.

Rolling Pin

It is best to use a heavy, smooth, and sturdy rolling pin with a high wood content. Rolling pins can also be made out of marble, stone or plastic, but the wooden ones are preferable, as they can handle the most amounts of excess flour. You should avoid wetting the rolling pin as much as possible. When choosing a rolling pin, keep size in mind; the longer the rolling pin, the more dough it will be able to handle. Always remember to flour both the rolling pin and the working space.

Ingredients
Preparation

*The following are
the basic ingredients and preparation tips
needed to make cookies.*

Butter

When butter is called for in a recipe, use unsalted butter unless directed otherwise. Butter should be used cold (straight out the refrigerator) and cut into small cubes, so that it will blend easier with flour, creating a crumb-like consistency. Some recipes call for butter at room temperature, so that it will blend easier when whisked with sugar and eggs, before the addition of flour.

Candy Decorations

There are an abundance of options for decorating cookies, using candies available at all grocery stores. Be creative and try using different ingredients: dried fruits, chocolates, and licorice, according to your personal tastes. Simply make sure that you have chosen edible items - the rest is up to you.

Eggs

Eggs add a rich texture to cookies and help to combine dry ingredients.
It is best to use fresh, medium-sized eggs at room temperature for most of these recipes.

Flour

Nearly all recipes in the book require all-purpose flour. It is very important to sift flour before measuring and using it in a recipe to allow for light and fluffy cookies. To measure, scoop it out of a flour bag or jar using a measuring cup, so that the flour mounts over the top of the cup. Sweep the back of a knife across the top of the measuring cup to level the flour. All types of flour should be stored in tightly sealed containers (I like wide ones for easy scooping) in a cool, dry cupboard. For recipes which call for all-purpose flour and baking powder together, you may substitute the same amount of flour with self-rising flour, and simply omit the baking powder. Several recipes call for different types of flours, such as cornmeal, potato flour, whole wheat flour, semolina, etc. These make for heavier, more compressed cookies. These flours are a great substitute for family and friends who suffer from celiac or allergies related to white flour.

Food Coloring

There are several forms of food coloring available in stores, namely powder, spread, liquid, markers, etc. Food coloring made from natural ingredients can be found at specialty stores, and I highly recommend using these as opposed to their processed counterparts. Pay attention to the manufacturers' expiration date on natural food colorings, as well as the storage instructions listed on the product.

Pure Vanilla Extract & Vanilla Beans

Vanilla is a plant belonging to the orchid family and its fruits are characterized by their aromatic seeds. Most vanilla beans come from Madagascar and are sold in specialty stores. To extract the vanilla from the vanilla bean, split it lengthwise using a sharp knife and use the back-side of the knife to scrape the black seeds out of the pod. Most of the recipes specify pure vanilla extract—you can tell a quality extract by its dark color and intense vanilla smell. For certain recipes it is preferable to use vanilla beans instead of extract, even though vanilla beans are expensive. The use of vanilla beans will give the cookies a dark spotted look.

Storing / Freezing

Most baked cookies may be stored in the freezer in an airtight container for 2-3 weeks. Cookies which contain cream or yeast and haven't been exposed to moisture may be stored for 4-7 days. Cookies which contain dairy products (besides butter) should be stored in the refrigerator. All cookies should be cooled before being stored in airtight containers.

Sugar

Most of the recipes in this book call for granulated white sugar and powdered sugar (also known as confectioners' sugar). However, a few of the recipes call for dark brown sugar or demerara sugar (golden brown), which provide texture and color. Sugar can be substituted or combined with other sweeteners, such as honey, maple, molasses or sugar substitutes for those with health or dietary concerns.

Rolling Dough

It is best to roll out dough on a clean, flat and dry surface area, large enough to accommodate the dough once it has been rolled out. The work space you roll out the dough on should always be lightly floured so that the dough does not stick to the surface. Don't use too much flour; otherwise the consistency of the dough is likely to change. If the dough has become too soft and warm and is difficult to use, place it in the refrigerator for a few minutes and then continue rolling. In general, chilled dough is easier to work with. That's why many of the recipes in this book specify that the dough should be refrigerated before using it.

Basic Recipes

Basic Butter Cookies

Nothing is better than
the oh-so-plain but oh-so-good
butter cookie that melts
in your mouth.

Ingredients

2⅓ cups all-purpose flour
1½ sticks (6 oz.) butter, cubed
¼ teaspoon salt
1 cup powdered sugar
1 tablespoon lemon zest
1 egg
1 teaspoon pure vanilla extract

Preparation

1. Using a stand mixer fitted with a paddle attachment, mix together the flour, butter, salt, powdered sugar and lemon zest until crumbs form.

2. Add the egg and vanilla extract and mix for 1 minute until all the ingredients are combined and dough forms.

3. Cover the dough in plastic wrap and refrigerate for 1 hour.

4. Preheat oven to 350°F. Working on a lightly floured surface, roll out dough to a thickness of about ⅛ inch. Using any cookie cutter of your choice, cut out rounds of the dough and transfer to a baking sheet lined with parchment paper, spacing 2 inches apart.

5. Bake for 22-25 minutes. Transfer to a cooling rack to cool completely.

6. Cookies can be stored for up to a week in an airtight container at room temperature.

~~~ **Playing around** ~~~

Glaze cookies by brushing them with an egg wash before baking (one lightly-beaten egg mixed with a teaspoon of water). Sprinkle sugar on top of each cookie.

MAKES 60 COOKIES

Basic Chocolate Cookies

This is the easiest chocolate cookie recipe around! Spruce it up by adding a half a cup of walnuts or any other type of nut of your choice.

Ingredients

2¼ cups all-purpose flour
1¾ sticks (7 oz.) butter, cubed
¼ teaspoon salt
1 cup powdered sugar
¾ cup cocoa powder
1 egg
1 tablespoon pure vanilla extract

Preparation

1. Using a stand mixer fitted with a paddle attachment, mix together the flour, butter, salt, powdered sugar and cocoa powder, until the dough forms a crumb-like texture.

2. Add the egg and vanilla extract and continue to mix for 1 minute, until all the ingredients are combined and dough is formed.

3. Wrap dough in plastic wrap and refrigerate for 1 hour.

4. Preheat oven to 350°F. Working on a lightly floured surface, roll out dough to a thickness of about ⅛ inch. Using any cookie cutter of your choice, cut out rounds of the dough and transfer to a baking sheet lined with parchment paper, spacing 2 inches apart.

5. Bake for 20-25 minutes. Transfer to a cooling rack to cool completely.

6. Cookies can be stored for up to a week in an airtight container at room temperature.

MAKES 60 COOKIES

Dairy-Free Cookies

This great easy-to-prepare cookie is ideal for a crowd, especially when you don't know whether anyone is allergic to dairy products.

Ingredients

3 cups all-purpose flour
¼ teaspoon salt
1 cup sugar
2 eggs
½ cup canola oil
1 tablespoon pure vanilla extract

Preparation

1. In a large bowl, mix together the flour, salt and sugar.

2. In a separate bowl, whisk together the eggs, oil, and vanilla extract.

3. Gradually add the wet mixture to the dry one and mix until all ingredients are combined.

4. Cover the bowl with plastic wrap and refrigerate for 1 hour.

5. Preheat oven to 350°F. Working on a lightly floured surface, roll out dough to a thickness of about ⅛ inch. Using any cookie cutter of your choice, cut out rounds of the dough and transfer to a baking sheet lined with parchment paper, spacing 2 inches apart.

6. Bake for 22-25 minutes. Transfer to a cooling rack to cool completely.

7. Cookies can be stored for up to a week in an airtight container at room temperature.

MAKES 60 COOKIES

Shortbread Cookies

These light and airy cookies are great to serve next to your morning coffee or tea.

Ingredients

1¾ sticks (7 oz.) butter, at room temperature

½ cup sugar

1 tablespoon pure vanilla extract

1 egg

3 cups all-purpose flour

¼ teaspoon salt

2 teaspoons baking powder

Preparation

1. Preheat oven to 300°F. Using a stand mixer fitted with a paddle attachment, mix together the butter, sugar and vanilla extract on medium speed for 4 minutes. Add the egg, reduce speed to low and then gradually add the flour, salt and baking powder, mixing until just combined.

2. Wrap dough in plastic wrap and refrigerate for 1 hour. Working on a lightly floured surface, roll out the dough to 1-inch thick. Place dough on a baking sheet lined with parchment paper.

3. Bake for 15-17 minutes until golden. Transfer to a cooling rack and cut shortbread into 2-inch squares. Allow to cool completely.

4. Cookies can be stored for up to a week in an airtight container at room temperature.

MAKES 40 COOKIES

French Meringue Kisses

The perfect little treat
to have in your cupboard,
as this recipe yields plenty.
Just make sure to keep them
in an airtight container,
otherwise these crisp cookies
may get soggy.

Ingredients

4 large egg whites, at room temperature
¼ teaspoon salt
½ cup sugar
¾ cup powdered sugar

Preparation

1. Preheat oven to 150°F. Using a stand mixer fitted with a whisk attachment, whisk together the egg whites and salt at medium speed for 4 minutes and gradually add the sugar.

2. Gradually add the powdered sugar while increasing speed, until stiff, glossy peaks form.

3. Transfer meringue to a pastry bag fitted with a round attachment. Pipe the meringue mixture onto a baking sheet lined with parchment paper. Each meringue should be about the size of a quarter.

4. Bake for 3 hours or until the meringue is hard and dry.

5. Cookies may be stored for up to 2 weeks in an airtight container at room temperature.

MAKES 120 COOKIES

Royal Icing

There are many toppings
to decorate your cookies with,
but none are as classic
as royal icing.

Ingredients

3 large egg whites, at room temperature
¼ teaspoon cream of tartar
4 cups powdered sugar

Preparation

1. In a large bowl, whisk together the egg whites and cream of tartar for 2 minutes until frothy.

2. Gradually add the powdered sugar and continue to whisk for another 2 minutes on high speed until the mixture is thick and shiny.

MAKES 3 2/3 CUPS

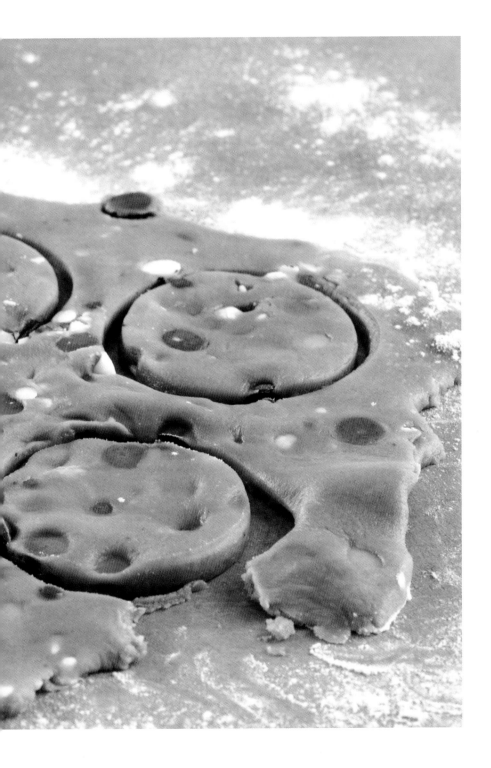

Classic Cookies

Chocolate Rugelach

Show someone how much
you care about them by making
them these chocolate rugelach
for Sunday brunch.
They will be thanking you all week.

Ingredients

2½ cups all-purpose flour
2½ sticks (10 oz.) butter, cubed
¼ cup powdered sugar
¼ teaspoon salt
10 oz. cream cheese, at room temperature
For the chocolate filling
1½ pounds dark chocolate, chopped
3½ sticks (14 oz.) butter, at room temperature
1 egg, beaten for glaze

Preparation

1. Using a stand mixer fitted with a paddle attachment, mix together the flour, butter, powdered sugar and salt on medium speed until the mixture has a crumb-like consistency. Add the cream cheese and mix for another 2 minutes until soft dough forms.

2. Divide the dough into four equal balls. Wrap each ball with plastic wrap and refrigerate for at least 2 hours.

3. *Make the filling:* Melt chocolate in a heatproof bowl, set over a pan of simmering water. Stir occasionally. Add the butter and stir until butter is incorporated. Remove from heat and allow mixture to cool to room temperature.

4. Working on a lightly floured surface with one ball of dough at a time (keep the remainder in the refrigerator), roll out dough to thickness of about ⅛ inch in a rectangular shape.

5. Preheat oven to 350°F. Spread a thin layer of the filling onto the dough. Using a sharp knife, cut the dough in half lengthwise, and then cut each ½ into smaller wedges. Starting at the outside edge of each wedge, roll up into a crescent shape. Transfer to a baking sheet lined with parchment paper, spacing 1 inch apart, and brush with beaten egg. Repeat with remaining dough. Bake for 22-25 minutes, until golden brown and cooked through.

6. Cookies can be stored in an airtight container at room temperature for up to 3 days.

～ Playing around ～

*Alternatives for the filling include
1½ cups of fruit jam, cinnamon sugar
(mixed in equal amounts),
ricotta cheese, or Nutella.*

MAKES 50 COOKIES

Madelaine Cookies

These traditional French cookies with a sponge cake texture are distinctive due to their shell shape, which comes from a special baking pan made just for these cookies.

Ingredients

3 eggs
¾ cup sugar
1 tablespoon honey
¼ cup milk
2 tablespoons pure vanilla extract
1¾ sticks (7 oz.) butter, melted
1½ cups all-purpose flour
1½ teaspoons baking powder
For baking
Madelaine pan mold

Preparation

1. Using a mixer fitted with a whisk attachment, mix together the eggs and sugar for about 5 minutes, until light and fluffy. Add the honey, milk, vanilla extract and butter, and whisk until all ingredients are combined. In a separate bowl, sift together the flour and baking powder.

2. Gradually add the flour to the wet mixture and whisk until the mixture is smooth.

3. Cover the bowl with plastic wrap and refrigerate for at least 30 minutes before baking.

4. Preheat oven to 350°F. Generously butter a Madelaine pan mold. (If using a silicon mold, there is no need to butter.)

5. Pour the chilled batter into the pan mold, filling each mold to the very top. Bake for 15 minutes, until a toothpick, placed in the center, comes out dry.

6. Allow to chill to room temperature before serving.

7. Cookies can be stored in an airtight container at room temperature for up to 1 week.

MAKES **20** COOKIES

Diamond Butter Cookies

The sugar on the rim
of these cookies sparkles
like diamonds, hence the name
Diamond Butter Cookies.

Ingredients

1¾ sticks (7 oz.) butter, cubed

2¾ cups all-purpose flour

1 cup powdered sugar

½ tablespoon lemon zest

¼ teaspoon salt

1 tablespoon pure vanilla extract

1 egg + 1 egg, beaten and mixed with
1 teaspoon water

1 cup sugar

Preparation

1. Using a stand mixer fitted with a paddle attachment mix together the butter, flour, powdered sugar, lemon zest and salt, until crumbs form. Add the vanilla extract and egg, and mix until the consistency is like dough.

2. Roll the dough into a 1-inch diameter log. If the dough is too soft, you can refrigerate for 15 minutes before rolling.

3. Place the dough log on a sheet of parchment paper and place in the freezer for about 15 minutes, until the dough has hardened.

4. Preheat oven to 350°F. Remove the dough from the freezer and brush with the egg wash. Roll the dough in the sugar, making sure that the sugar sticks to the dough and that the dough is generously covered in sugar (some will fall off during baking).

5. Using a sharp knife, cut the dough into ⅛ inch slices and place on a baking sheet, spacing 2 inches apart.

6. Bake for 12-15 minutes, until pale gold in color. Allow to cool completely on a cooling rack before serving.

7. Cookies can be stored in an airtight container at room temperature for up to 1 week.

MAKES **100** COOKIES

Linzer Sables

Linzer sables are traditionally
made with strawberry jam,
but get creative and use your own
homemade seasonal jam to give
these cookies a personal touch.

Ingredients

2 sticks (8 oz.) butter, at room temperature
1 cup sugar
2 eggs
1 teaspoon pure vanilla extract
4 cups all-purpose flour
2 teaspoons baking powder
¼ teaspoon salt
1 cup strawberry jam
½ cup powdered sugar

Preparation

1. Using a stand mixer fitted with a paddle attachment, mix together the butter and sugar for 2 minutes at medium speed until the mixture is light and fluffy. Add the eggs, one at a time, and mix until they are incorporated. Add in the vanilla extract and continue mixing.

2. Gradually add the flour, baking powder, and salt until dough forms. Do not over mix. Cover the ball of dough with plastic wrap and refrigerate for 1 hour.

3. Preheat oven to 350°F. Working on a lightly floured surface, roll out the dough to ¼ inch thick. Using a 2-inch scalloped (or round) cookie cutter, cut out as many cookies as you can and place cookies on a baking sheet lined with parchment paper, spacing 1 inch apart.

4. Using the end of a piping tip, cut out small circles from the centers of half of the cookies.

5. Bake for 15 minutes until golden. Transfer to a cooling rack and allow cookies to cool completely.

6. Place ½ teaspoon of jam onto each whole cookie (the ones without the holes) and then close the sandwich with one of the cookies with a hole in it. Sprinkle with powdered sugar before serving.

7. Cookies may be stored for up to 1 week in an airtight container at room temperature.

MAKES 30 COOKIE SANDWICHES

Red Currant Financiers

Financiers,
also known as friands,
are delicious French tea cakes that
are easy to make and really make an
impression. You can use a teaspoon
to transfer the batter into the
financier pan mold, but the pastry
bag simply makes the work
at lot easier.

Ingredients

1 cup all-purpose flour
¾ cup ground almonds
2¾ cups powdered sugar
10 egg whites
1¾ sticks (7 oz.) butter, melted
1 cup red currants

Preparation

1. Using a mixer, whisk together the flour, ground almonds, and powdered sugar. Gradually add the egg whites and butter beat for about 2 minutes. Cover the bowl with plastic wrap and refrigerate for at least 1 hour.

2. Preheat oven to 340°F. Pour the batter into a pastry bag fitted with a round tip.

3. Squeeze the batter into the financier molds, filling each one about ¾ full. Place 2-3 red currants in each mold.

4. Bake for 22-25 minutes until a toothpick, placed in the center, comes out dry. Transfer to a cooling rack to cool slightly. Serve warm.

5. Cookies can be stored in an airtight container at room temperature for up to 3 days.

MAKES 12 COOKIES

Raisin & Rum Cookies

Raisins and rum are a natural combination that works wonders in these tasty cookies.

Ingredients

⅓ cup dark raisins

½ cup light rum

1¾ cups powdered sugar

2¼ cups all-purpose flour

3 eggs + 2 egg yolks

1¾ sticks (7 oz.) butter, melted and cooled

1 tablespoon pure vanilla extract

For frosting

1 cup powdered sugar

1 tablespoon rum

Preparation

1. Place the raisins and rum in a small bowl, and allow to stand for at least 30 minutes, until the raisins soak up the rum. Strain raisins before adding to mixture.

2. In a large bowl, sift together the powdered sugar and flour. Add the eggs, egg yolks, butter, vanilla extract and raisins. Mix until all ingredients are combined well and refrigerate batter for 1 hour.

3. Preheat oven to 350°F.

4. Drop a heaped tablespoon of batter onto a baking sheet lined with parchment paper, spacing 2 inches apart. Bake for 10-12 minutes until cookies are golden brown. Transfer cookies to a cooling rack.

5. *Make the frosting:* In a large bowl, whisk the powdered sugar and rum together until the mixture is thick and white. Spread the frosting evenly onto each cookie and return to the oven for 10 seconds, just long enough for the frosting to harden.

6. Cookies may be stored for up to 1 week in an airtight container at room temperature.

MAKES 20 COOKIES

Mint Chocolate Cookies

The combination of mint and chocolate has worked wonders in ice cream; with these cookies the combination proves itself once again.

Ingredients

1½ cups all-purpose flour
¼ teaspoon salt
1 tablespoon baking powder
10 oz. mint chocolate, coarsely chopped
1 tablespoon pure mint extract
¾ stick (3 oz.) butter, room temperature
1 cup sugar
2 eggs

Preparation

1. In a large bowl, sift together the flour, salt and baking powder.

2. Melt mint chocolate in a heatproof bowl, set over a pan of simmering water. Stir occasionally. Add mint extract, stir, and remove from heat. Allow to chill for 10 minutes.

3. Using a mixer fitted with whisk attachment, whisk the butter and sugar for 2 minutes on medium speed until light and fluffy. Add the eggs one by one and continue mixing. Gradually add the melted chocolate and whisk for 1 minute until the chocolate is combined.

4. Gradually add the dry ingredients and mix until all ingredients are combined. Cover bowl with plastic wrap and refrigerate for 1 hour.

5. Preheat oven to 350°F. Using a 1½-inch ice cream scoop, drop dough onto baking sheets lined with parchment paper, spacing about 2 inches apart.

6. Bake for 12-15 minutes. Allow to cool on a cooling rack before serving.

7. Cookies may be stored in an airtight container at room temperature for up to 3 days.

MAKES 45 COOKIES

Almond Lace Cookies

The short list of ingredients required for these crispy, nutty and sweet cookies makes them the perfect treat to make when you are low on groceries.

Ingredients

2 egg whites

1 cup powdered sugar

1 teaspoon almond liqueur, such as Amaretto (almond-flavored liqueur)

2 cups almond slivers

Preparation

1. Preheat the oven to 350°F. In a large bowl, mix together the egg whites, powdered sugar, and almond liqueur, making sure not to over mix (no foam should appear).

2. Add the almond slivers and mix until the almonds are well covered.

3. Scoop out a heaped teaspoon of the batter and smooth it out on a baking sheet lined with parchment paper. Repeat with the rest of the batter, leaving a 1½-inch space between cookies.

4. Bake for about 12-15 minutes, until pale gold in color. Cool on baking sheet on a cooling rack. Decorate cookies with powdered sugar before serving.

5. Cookies can be stored in an airtight container at room temperature for up to 1 week.

MAKES 20 COOKIES

Florentines

These crisp Italian almond treats
are not your average cookie.

Ingredients

3 cups all-purpose flour

1 tablespoon baking powder

1¾ sticks (7 oz.) butter, at room temperature

¼ teaspoon salt

1 cup powdered sugar

1 tablespoon orange zest

1 egg

1 teaspoon pure vanilla extract

For the top layer

1½ cups sugar

1 stick (4 oz.) butter

3 tablespoons honey

¼ teaspoon salt

¾ cup heavy cream

14 oz. almond slivers

Preparation

1. Using a stand mixer fitted with a paddle attachment, mix the flour, baking powder, butter, salt, powdered sugar and orange zest on medium speed for 3 minutes until the mixture has a crumb-like texture. Add the egg and vanilla extract and mix for 1 minute until dough is formed. Wrap the dough in plastic wrap and refrigerate for 1 hour.

2. Preheat oven to 350°F. Working on a lightly floured surface, roll out dough to a thickness of about ⅛ inch. Transfer dough to a baking sheet lined with parchment paper and bake for 10-12 minutes.

3. *Make the top layer:* Place the sugar, butter, honey, salt and heavy cream in a small saucepan over low heat for 5 minutes and then mix in the almond slivers and remove from heat.

4. Pour almond mixture evenly over the baked cookie sheet and smooth out using a spatula. Reduce oven temperature to 330°F and return cookies to oven for another 12-15 minutes. Make sure not to over bake.

5. Transfer to a cooling rack. Once completely cooled, cut out 1-inch square cookies.

6. Cookies may be stored for up to 1 week in an airtight container at room temperature.

MAKES **50** COOKIES

Almond Horn Cookies

These horseshoe-shaped cookies
may not bring you good luck,
but they will definitely
put a smile on your face.

Ingredients

1½ cups all-purpose flour

1 cup ground almonds

½ cup ground skinless hazelnuts,
finely ground in a food processor

2 sticks (8 oz.) butter, at room temperature

¼ teaspoon salt

½ cup powdered sugar + ½ cup for decoration

1 egg yolk

1 tablespoon pure vanilla extract

Preparation

1. Using a stand mixer fitted with a paddle attachment, mix together the flour, ground almonds, ground hazelnuts, butter, salt, and powdered sugar on medium speed for 2 minutes. Add the egg yolk and vanilla extract and mix for 1 minute until dough is formed. Wrap the dough in plastic wrap and refrigerate for 2 hours.

2. Preheat oven to 320°F. Roll 1 tablespoon of dough into a 4-inch-long log and then gently shape into a horseshoe. Repeat process with remaining dough. Transfer cookies to a baking sheet lined with parchment paper, spacing 2 inches apart.

3. Bake for 18-20 minutes until cookies are pale gold in color. Transfer to a cooling rack until completely cooled. Decorate with powdered sugar before serving.

4. Cookies may be stored for up to a week in an airtight container at room temperature.

MAKES 35 COOKIES

Caramel Nut Bars

These bars call for pecans, but you can replace the pecans with the same amount of any other nut.

Ingredients

2 cups all-purpose flour

¾ cup ground almonds

1½ sticks (6 oz.) butter, cubed

¼ teaspoon salt

¼ cup powdered sugar

1 egg

1 tablespoon pure vanilla extract

For the topping

3 cups sugar

1½ cups heavy cream, at room temperature

¾ stick (3 oz.) butter, at room temperature

1 tablespoon pure vanilla extract

1½ pounds whole pecans

Preparation

1. *Make the crust:* Using a stand mixer fitted with a paddle attachment, mix together the flour, ground almonds, butter, salt, and powdered sugar for 2 minutes on medium speed until the mixture has a crumb-like texture. Add the egg and vanilla extract and mix for 1 minute until dough is formed. Wrap the dough in plastic wrap and refrigerate for 1 hour.

2. Preheat oven to 350°F. Working on a lightly floured surface, roll out dough to a thickness of about ⅛ inch. Transfer dough to a baking sheet lined with parchment paper and bake for 12-15 minutes. Transfer to a cooling rack and allow the baked crust to cool completely.

3. *Make the topping:* Melt the sugar in small saucepan over low heat until the sugar turns into a light caramel. Slowly pour in the heavy cream while stirring constantly. Add the butter and vanilla extract and cook for 1 minute while stirring, until the mixture becomes toffee-like. Add the pecans, cook for 1 minute, and then remove from heat.

4. Pour pecan mixture evenly over the baked crust and press down gently using a spatula. Reduce oven temperature to 340°F and return mixture to oven for another 4-6 minutes. Transfer to a cooling rack. Once completely cooled, cut out 1-inch x 2-inch rectangular cookies.

5. Bars may be stored for up to 1 week in an airtight container at room temperature.

MAKES
60
BARS

Lemon Bars

Ingredients

2½ cups all-purpose flour

1½ sticks (6 oz.) butter, cubed

½ cup powdered sugar

¼ teaspoon salt

1 tablespoon lemon zest

1 egg

1 teaspoon pure vanilla extract

For the filling

7 gelatin leaves

2½ cups lemon juice

2 tablespoons lemon zest

10 eggs + 10 egg yolks

2⅔ cups sugar

4 sticks (16 oz.) butter, cubed

For decoration

½ cup powdered sugar

For baking

One 16 inch x 16 inch baking dish

Preparation

1. **Make the crust:** Using a stand mixer fitted with a paddle attachment, mix together the flour, butter, powdered sugar, salt and lemon zest on medium speed for 2 minutes until the mixture has a crumb-like consistency. Add the egg and vanilla extract and mix for 1 minute until dough is formed. Cover the dough in plastic wrap and refrigerate for 1 hour.

2. Preheat oven to 350°F. Working on a lightly floured surface, roll out dough to a thickness of about ⅛ inch. Transfer dough to a 16-inch x 16-inch baking dish lined with parchment paper and bake for 12-15 minutes. Transfer to a cooling rack and allow crust to cool completely.

3. **Make the filling:** Place the gelatin leaves in a bowl filled with cold water for about 5 minutes until leaves have softened and then strain the remaining water, using a fine sieve.

4. In a small saucepan, heat the lemon juice, lemon zest, eggs, egg yolks, sugar and butter on low heat, while constantly stirring, until the mixture has a creamy texture. It's essential to stir the mixture constantly; otherwise the eggs will turn into scrambled eggs.

5. Remove saucepan from heat and add the softened gelatin leaves. Stir until the gelatin has dissolved. Pass the entire mixture through a fine sieve in order to remove the lemon zest and other hard particles.

6. Pour the filling over the crust and refrigerate for at least 2 hours or until the lemon cream has become stiff.

7. Using a sharp knife, cut out 1-inch x 2-inch rectangles. Decorate with powdered sugar before serving.

8. Bars may be stored for 2 days in an airtight container in the refrigerator.

MAKES 50 BARS

good times

lovely

fabulous

Cookies for Kids

Nutella Thumbprints

Your kids will not be able to resist these cookies for two reasons: They are so much fun to make and they contain Nutella - no need to say more.

Ingredients

2 cups all-purpose flour
¼ teaspoon salt
1¾ sticks (7 oz.) butter, cold and cut into cubes
1 cup powdered sugar
1 egg yolk
1 tablespoon pure vanilla extract
For the filling
1 cup Nutella hazelnut spread

Preparation

1. Using a mixer fitted with a paddle attachment, mix together the flour, salt, butter and powdered sugar on medium speed for 2 minutes until the mixture has a crumb-like texture. Add the egg yolk and vanilla extract, and continue mixing for 1 minute until dough is formed. Wrap dough in plastic wrap and refrigerate for 1 hour.

2. Preheat oven to 340°F. Roll the dough into 1-inch balls and place onto baking sheets lined with parchment paper, spacing about 2 inches apart. Press down the center of each ball using your thumb.

3. Bake for 12-15 minutes until golden. Transfer to a cooling rack to cool completely.

4. Fill each center with Nutella, using a teaspoon or a pastry bag.

5. Cookies may be stored in an airtight container at room temperature for up to 1 week.

MAKES 50 COOKIES

Milk Chocolate & Cornflake Fingers

These cookies are the perfect treat to have around the house for when your kids come home from school. They will be smiling all the way to their rooms to do homework.

Ingredients

5⅓ cups milk chocolate, coarsely chopped
1¾ sticks (7 oz.) butter
1¼ pounds (20 oz.) unfrosted cornflakes, crumbled

Preparation

1. Melt chocolate and butter in a heatproof bowl, set over a pan of simmering water. Stir occasionally. Add the cornflakes, stir and remove from heat.

2. Pour mixture onto a baking sheet lined with parchment paper. Cover mixture with another sheet of parchment paper and use a rolling pin to evenly distribute the mixture onto the baking sheet. Refrigerate for 1 hour.

3. Remove from refrigerator and cut into 1-inch x 2-inch rectangles.

4. Cookies can be stored in an airtight container in the refrigerator for up to 1 week.

～ Playing around ～

You can replace the cornflakes with any cereal of your choice, just make sure to use a cereal that it is not sweetened or frosted, otherwise your cookies will be too sweet.

MAKES 30 COOKIES

Sprinkled Chocolate Balls

The trick of preventing these balls from sticking to your hands when rolling them is to coat your hands with a bit of canola oil - they will slide right off.

Ingredients

½ stick (2 oz.) butter
½ cup milk
½ cup heavy cream
½ cup sugar
½ cup cocoa powder
5 oz. dark chocolate, broken up into cubes
7 oz. graham crackers, crumbled
1 cup colored sprinkles

Preparation

1. In a medium saucepan, heat the butter, milk, heavy cream and sugar until the butter has completely melted and sugar has dissolved. Add the cocoa powder and mix until all ingredients are combined. Remove from heat.

2. Add the chocolate cubes to the warm liquid mixture and mix until the chocolate has melted. Add the graham cracker crumbs and stir to combine.

3. Place the mixture into a bowl and cover with plastic wrap. Refrigerate for about 2 hours, or until the mixture has set and is completely cold.

4. Using your hands or a spoon, create golf ball-sized balls (or any size of your liking) out of the chocolate mixture.

5. Place the sprinkles on a flat plate and roll each of the chocolate balls onto the sprinkles, applying enough pressure so that the sprinkles stick.

6. Cookies can be stored in an airtight container at room temperature for up to 1 week.

~~~ Playing around ~~~

Make the same cookies for adults by replacing the sprinkles with cocoa powder, crushed peanuts, chopped pistachios, or roasted coconut.

MAKES **20** BALLS

Chocolate & Graham Cracker Cookies

To crumble the graham crackers more easily, you can either use a food processor or place them in a zip lock bag and use a rolling pin to lightly bang the bag over the kitchen counter.

Ingredients

5 oz. milk chocolate

¾ stick (3 oz.) butter

¼ cup chocolate milk

2 tablespoons sugar

1 tablespoon pure vanilla extract

7 oz. graham crackers, crumbled

Preparation

1. In a small saucepan, heat the chocolate, butter, chocolate milk, sugar and vanilla extract on low heat until all ingredients are combined well. Remove from heat and add graham cracker crumbs. Allow to chill to room temperature.

2. Place a large sheet of plastic wrap on a working surface and pour the mixture onto the plastic wrap. Roll into a 3-inch log and wrap with the plastic wrap. Refrigerate for 2 hours until hardened.

3. Remove the plastic wrap and use a sharp knife to slice ¼-inch wide cookies.

4. Cookies can be stored in an airtight container in the refrigerator for up to 1 week.

~~~ **Playing around** ~~~

If you don't have graham crackers in your cupboard, you can replace them using the same amount of any cookie you like. Even the most simple butter cookies will work like a charm.

MAKES 20 COOKIES

Mini Marshmallow Cookies

Because these cookies contain marshmallow, they tend to spread out a lot during baking. So make sure to give each cookie plenty of space.

Ingredients

¾ cup (5 oz.) dark chocolate, coarsely chopped
1½ cups all-purpose flour
1 tablespoon baking powder
¼ teaspoon salt
1 stick (4 oz.) butter
1 cup sugar
2 eggs
1⅓ cups mini marshmallows

Preparation

1. Melt chocolate in a heatproof bowl, set over a pan of simmering water. Stir occasionally. Remove from heat and allow chocolate to cool to room temperature.

2. In a large bowl, sift together the flour, baking powder, and salt. Using a mixer fitted with a whisk attachment, mix together the butter and sugar on medium speed for 2 minutes until light and fluffy. Add the eggs, one by one, and then add the melted chocolate and continue mixing. Gradually add the flour mixture and continue mixing for 1 minute until all ingredients are combined well.

3. Preheat oven to 320°F. Using a 1½-inch ice cream scoop, drop dough onto baking sheets lined with parchment paper, spacing about 3½ inches apart. Gently press 4-5 mini marshmallows onto the top of each cookie.

4. Bake for 12-15 minutes. Cool on sheet on a cooling rack.

5. Cookies can be stored in an airtight container at room temperature for up to 1 week.

MAKES 30 COOKIES

Cinnamon Twists

These cinnamon twists
are a blast to make with kids
because all that is really involved
is twisting and sprinkling—
two activities your kids will love!

Ingredients

1 cup sugar

½ cup cinnamon

One 17.25-oz. package frozen puff pastry
(2 sheets), thawed

1 egg, beaten

Preparation

1. Preheat oven to 400°F. In a small bowl, mix together the sugar and cinnamon.

2. Brush the pastry sheets with the egg and sprinkle with the cinnamon sugar mixture. Cut each sheet of pastry crosswise into strips, ¾-inch wide.

3. Twist each strip and place on a baking sheet lined with parchment paper, spacing the strips 1 inch apart.

4. Bake for 10-12 minutes until golden and crisp. Transfer to a cooling rack to cool completely.

5. Cookies may be stored in an airtight container at room temperature for up to 1 week.

MAKES **60** TWISTS

Homemade Ice Cream Sandwiches

Cookies are a treat
all on their own,
but when a scoop of your
favorite chocolate is placed
in between two cookies,
you're in for a special treat!

Ingredients

1 cup all-purpose flour

⅓ cup cornstarch

⅓ cup cocoa powder

½ cup shredded coconut

1¼ sticks (5 oz.) butter, at room temperature

1 cup powdered sugar

For sandwich

15 scoops store-bought ice cream

Preparation

1. In a large bowl, mix together the flour, cornstarch, cocoa powder, and shredded coconut.

2. Using a mixer fitted with a whisk attachment, mix together the butter and powdered sugar for 2 minutes on medium speed until light and fluffy. Gradually add the dry ingredients and mix until all ingredients are combined. Cover the dough in plastic wrap and refrigerate for 1 hour.

3. Preheat oven to 340°F. Working on a lightly floured surface, roll out dough to a thickness of about ⅛ inch. Using a sharp knife, cut out 3-inch squares and place them on a baking sheet lined with parchment paper, spacing about 1 inch apart.

4. Bake for 10-12 minutes. Allow to cool completely on a cooling rack before making sandwiches.

5. ***Make the ice cream sandwich:*** Place a heaped scoop of ice cream on one cookie and close the sandwich with a second cookie. Serve immediately.

6. Cookies sandwiches can be prepared up to a week in advance and kept in the freezer in an airtight container.

MAKES
15
COOKIE
SANDWICHES

Cookies

These easy-to-make cookies
are a great party favor
to give away at your child's
next birthday party.

Ingredients

2 sticks (8 oz.) butter, at room temperature
1 cup sugar
¾ cup brown sugar
2 eggs
3¼ cups all-purpose flour
¼ teaspoon salt
1 teaspoon baking soda
1½ cups M&M's

Preparation

1. Using a stand mixer fitted with a paddle attachment, mix the butter and both sugars together on medium speed until pale and fluffy. Add the eggs, one at a time, and continue to mix for 1 minute.

2. Gradually add the flour, salt and baking soda and continue mixing until combined. Stir in the M&M's.

3. Preheat oven to 350°F. Dip a tablespoon in water, scoop out the dough, and drop onto baking sheets lined with parchment paper, spacing about 2 inches apart.

4. Bake cookies for 12-15 minutes, until golden brown.

5. Cookies can be stored in an airtight container at room temperature for up to 1 week.

MAKES
30
COOKIES

Peanut Butter & Jelly Cookie Sandwich

Although these cookies
are meant for kids,
grown-ups will also enjoy
the trip down memory lane.

Ingredients

1¼ sticks (5 oz.) butter, at room temperature
½ cup smooth peanut butter
1 tablespoon strawberry jam
1 cup sugar
2 eggs
1 teaspoon pure vanilla extract
1½ cups all-purpose flour
1 teaspoon baking powder
For the filling
½ cup strawberry jam

Preparation

1. Using a mixer fitted with a whisk attachment, mix together the butter, peanut butter, strawberry jam and sugar on medium speed for 3 minutes, until the mixture is fluffy. Add the eggs, one by one, and then add the vanilla extract and continue mixing.

2. Gradually add in the flour and baking powder, and continue to mix for another 2 minutes until all ingredients are combined and a soft dough forms. Cover the bowl with plastic wrap and refrigerate for 1 hour.

3. Preheat oven to 340°F. Working on a lightly floured surface, roll out the dough to ⅛ inch thick. Using a 2-inch round cookie cutter, cut out cookies and place on a baking sheet, spacing 1 inch apart.

4. Bake for 12-15 minutes. Transfer to a cooling rack to cool completely.

5. *Make the sandwich:* Spread about 2 teaspoons of strawberry jam over half of the cookies on their flat side; place a second cookie on top of the jam-covered ones to create sandwiches.

6. Cookie sandwiches can be stored in an airtight container at room temperature for up to 3 days.

MAKES 35 COOKIE SANDWICHES

Pretzel Cookies

Kids love pretzels of all shapes and sizes, so why not try to make a pretzel cookie?

Ingredients

2⅔ cups all-purpose flour
1 tablespoon lemon zest
1¼ cups powdered sugar
¼ teaspoon salt
1¾ sticks (7 oz.) butter
1 tablespoon baking powder
2 eggs
2 tablespoons pure vanilla extract
For decoration
1 egg yolk
1 teaspoon white vinegar
½ cup sanding sugar

Preparation

1. Using a stand mixer fitted with a paddle attachment, mix together the flour, lemon zest, sugar, salt, butter and baking powder on medium speed for 3 minutes until the mixture has a crumb-like texture. Add the eggs, one by one, then add the vanilla extract and continue to mix for 1 minute, until all the ingredients are combined and a ball of dough is formed.

2. Wrap the ball of dough in plastic wrap and refrigerate for 1 hour.

3. Preheat oven to 340°F. Remove plastic wrap and divide the dough evenly into three parts. Roll dough into ¾-inch balls. Roll each ball into a 6-inch log and twist into the shape of a pretzel. Place on a baking sheet lined with parchment paper, spacing 1 inch apart.

4. *Make the decoration:* In a small bowl, combine the egg yolk and white vinegar. Brush each pretzel with the egg mixture and generously sprinkle on sanding sugar.

5. Bake for 22-25 minutes, until golden and crisp. Transfer to a cooling rack to cool completely.

6. Cookies may be stored in an airtight container at room temperature for up to 1 week.

MAKES **30** COOKIES

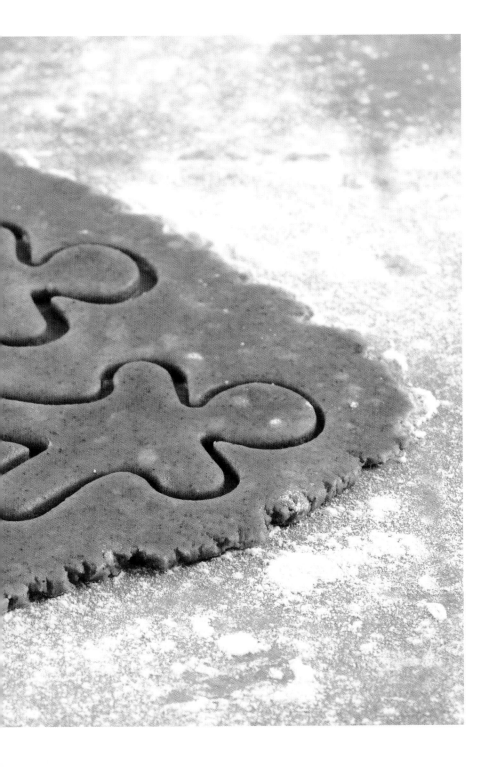

Cookies for Occasions

Christmas Meringue Snow Sandwiches

Make these cookies for up to 3 weeks before Christmas and store them in the freezer. When the family starts to fill up the house, you'll be all prepared with these sweet little treats.

Ingredients

4 egg whites, at room temperature
¼ teaspoon salt
½ cup sugar
¾ cup powdered sugar

For the white chocolate ganache
1½ cups heavy cream
16 oz. white chocolate, coarsely chopped
1 tablespoon brandy

Preparation

1. Preheat oven to 170°F. Using a mixer fitted with a whisk attachment, mix together the egg whites and salt on medium speed for 2 minutes. Gradually add the sugar, while whisking continuously. Add the powdered sugar and continue whisking until stiff, glossy peaks form.

2. Transfer mixture to a pastry bag fitted with a star tip and pipe the mixture onto a baking sheet lined with parchment paper in the shape of drops.

3. Bake for 3 hours until the meringue is hard and completely dry from within. Allow to cool to room temperature before making sandwiches.

4. ***Make the chocolate ganache:*** In a small saucepan, heat the heavy cream on low heat until just barely simmering. Remove from heat and add the white chocolate. Stir until the chocolate has completely melted. Add the brandy and refrigerate for at least one hour until the ganache hardens.

5. ***Make the sandwiches:*** Place a ½ teaspoon of ganache on the smooth side of one meringue and close the sandwich with a second meringue. Cookies can be kept in an airtight container in the freezer for up to 3 weeks.

MAKES **60** SANDWICHES

Baby Shower Cookies

MAKES
18
COOKIES

These cookies are not only great party favors to give guests at your next baby shower; decorating them is also a great activity for the shower itself. Just prepare the cookies ahead of time, put the frosting and all the candy for decoration in the center of the table, and allow guests to create their own "baby faces".

Ingredients

2½ cups all-purpose flour

1 teaspoon baking soda

¼ teaspoon salt

½ cup cocoa powder

1¼ sticks (5 oz.) butter, at room temperature

½ cup light brown sugar

⅔ cup honey

For the frosting

4 egg whites

4 cups powdered sugar

For decoration

Licorice, M&Ms and caramel popcorn

Preparation

1. In a large bowl, sift together the flour, baking soda, salt and cocoa powder. Using a stand mixer fitted with a paddle attachment, mix together the butter and brown sugar on medium speed for 3-4 minutes until pale and fluffy. Add the honey and mix for 1 minute.

2. Gradually add the flour mixture to the mixer and mix for another 2 minutes, until all ingredients are combined and dough forms. Wrap the dough in plastic wrap and refrigerate for 30 minutes.

3. Preheat oven to 350°F. Remove dough from the refrigerator and roll out the dough in between 2 sheets of parchment paper to a thickness of about ⅛ inch. Using a 4-inch round cookie cutter, cut out rounds of the dough and transfer to a baking sheet lined with parchment paper, spacing 2 inches apart.

4. Bake for 12-15 minutes until golden. Cool completely on a cooling rack.

5. *Make the frosting:* In a large bowl, whisk the egg whites for about 1 minute and then gradually add the powdered sugar. Continue to whisk until the mixture is smooth.

6. Once cookies have completely cooled, brush the frosting evenly onto each cookie and decorate the cookies using the M&Ms for the eyes and nose, licorice for the mouth and popcorn for the hair.

7. Wait 20 minutes for the frosting to dry and for the decorations to set before serving.

New Year's Pop Rock Cookies

MAKES **20** COOKIES

New Year's Eve parties are generally filled with sparklers and sparkling wine, so why not throw in a sparkling dessert to please the crowd?

Ingredients

2½ cups all-purpose flour

½ teaspoon salt

1 teaspoon baking powder

½ teaspoon baking soda

1¾ sticks (7 oz.) butter, at room temperature

1¼ cups powdered sugar

2 egg yolks

1 tablespoon pure vanilla extract

¼ cup + ½ cup popping candy, such as pop rocks

For icing

1 large egg white, at room temperature

¼ teaspoon cream of tartar

1⅓ cups powdered sugar

Preparation

1. In a large bowl, sift together the flour, salt, baking powder and baking soda. Using a mixer fitted with a whisk attachment, mix together the butter and powdered sugar on medium speed for 2 minutes until light and fluffy. Add the egg yolks, one at a time. Add the vanilla extract and continue mixing.

2. Reduce mixer speed to low and gradually add the dry ingredients. Continue mixing for another 2 minutes until all ingredients are combined and dough forms. Add ¼ cup of popping candy and stir in with a wooden spoon.

3. Preheat oven to 340°F. Wet your hands slightly and roll the dough into 1½-inch balls. Place them onto baking sheets lined with parchment paper, gently pressing them down and spacing 3 inches apart.

4. Bake for 18-20 minutes until golden. Transfer to a cooling rack to cool completely.

5. *Make the icing:* In a large bowl, whisk together the egg white and cream of tartar for 2 minutes until frothy. Gradually add in the powdered sugar and continue whisking for another 2 minutes on high speed until the mixture is thick and shiny.

6. Spread a tablespoon of the icing onto each cookie and sprinkle the cookies with the remaining popping candy. Allow icing to harden before serving.

7. Cookies may be stored in an airtight container at room temperature for up to 3 days.

Gingerbread Man Cookies

MAKES **20** COOKIES

No cookie says Christmas more than the gingerbread man. Place these cookies in the freezer for 10 minutes before baking, and those little men will keep their shape better.

Ingredients

3 cups all-purpose flour

¼ teaspoon baking soda

½ teaspoon baking powder

½ teaspoon salt

1 teaspoon cinnamon

½ teaspoon ground nutmeg

1 teaspoon ground ginger

¼ teaspoon ground cloves

¾ stick (3 oz.) butter, at room temperature

⅓ cup molasses

1½ cups dark brown sugar, packed

1 egg

For decoration

Royal icing (see recipe page 23)

Candies, raisins and/or miniature semi-sweet chocolate chips for decorating

Preparation

1. In a large bowl, sift together the flour, baking soda, baking powder, salt, cinnamon, nutmeg, ginger and cloves.

2. Using a mixer fitted with a paddle attachment, mix together the butter, molasses and brown sugar on medium speed for 2 minutes, until the mixture is fluffy. Add the egg and continue mixing.

3. Reduce mixer speed to low and gradually add the dry ingredients. Continue mixing for another 2 minutes until all ingredients are combined well and dough forms. Wrap dough in plastic wrap and refrigerate for 1 hour.

4. Preheat oven to 340°F. Remove plastic wrap and working on a well-floured surface, roll out the dough to ⅛ inch thick. Using a gingerbread man cookie cutter, cut out cookies and place on a baking sheet, spacing 1 inch apart.

5. Bake for 10-12 minutes. Transfer to a cooling rack to cool completely. Decorate cookies with royal icing and candies as desired.

6. Cookies may be stored in an airtight container at room temperature for up to 2 days.

Halloween Pumpkin Cookies

These cookies are soft and moist, almost like perfect little pumpkin cakes. Why not serve them instead of candy?

Ingredients

2½ cups all-purpose flour

1 teaspoon baking powder

¼ teaspoon salt

1 tablespoon cinnamon

½ teaspoon ground nutmeg

¼ teaspoon ground allspice

1 stick (4 oz.) butter, at room temperature

¼ cup honey

1 cup brown sugar

1 cup canned pumpkin

1 egg

⅓ cup buttermilk

Preparation

1. In a large bowl, sift together the flour, baking powder, salt, cinnamon, nutmeg, and allspice.

2. Using a mixer fitted with a paddle attachment, mix the butter, honey, brown sugar and canned pumpkin on medium speed for 3 minutes, until the mixture is fluffy.

3. Add the egg and then alternately add the dry ingredients and the buttermilk. Continue mixing until all ingredients are combined and dough forms. Wrap dough in plastic wrap and refrigerate for 3 hours.

4. Preheat oven to 350°F. Using a 1½-inch ice cream scoop , drop dough onto baking sheets lined with parchment paper, spacing about 2 inches apart.

5. Bake for 18-20 minutes until golden. Transfer to a cooling rack to cool completely before serving

6. Cookies may be stored in an airtight container at room temperature for up to 1 week.

MAKES 35 COOKIES

Passover Cookies

Wheat flour is restricted during the Jewish holiday of Passover, so these cookies are the perfect solution. They are also great for those who suffer from celiac.

Ingredients

5 egg whites

¼ teaspoon salt

2 cups sugar

1 cup powdered sugar

5½ cups shredded coconut

2 tablespoons potato flour

2 teaspoons pure vanilla extract

For baking

80 paper cupcake liners

Preparation

1. Using a mixer fitted with a whisk attachment, mix together the egg whites and salt on high speed for 2 minutes. Gradually add the sugar and powdered sugar and continue whisking until stiff, glossy peaks form.

2. Using a flexible spatula, gently fold in the coconut and potato flour, and add the vanilla extract. Do not over fold.

3. Preheat oven to 350°F. Transfer mixture to pastry bag and pipe mixture into cupcake liners, filling them ¾ full. Place the filled cupcake liners onto a baking sheet.

4. Bake for 40-45 minutes, until cookies have hardened and are golden.

5. Cookies can be stored in an airtight container at room temperature for up to 1 week.

MAKES 80 COOKIES

Fourth of July Cookies

MAKES
60
COOKIES

These star-shaped red, white and blue cookies will help create a very festive atmosphere at your next Fourth of July summer bash.

Ingredients

3 cups all-purpose flour

½ teaspoon baking soda

¼ teaspoon salt

¾ cup hazelnuts, skinned and ground in a food processor

1¾ sticks (7 oz.) butter, at room temperature

1½ cups powdered sugar

2 eggs

2 tablespoons rum extract

For decoration

1 cup powdered sugar

1 tablespoon light corn syrup

1 tablespoon lemon juice

Red and blue food coloring

Red and blue colored sugar

Preparation

1. In a large bowl, sift together the flour, baking soda, salt and ground hazelnuts. Using a mixer fitted with a paddle attachment, mix together the butter and powdered sugar on medium speed for 2 minutes, until light and fluffy. Add the eggs, one at a time. Add the rum extract and continue mixing.

2. Reduce mixer speed to low and gradually add the dry ingredients. Continue mixing for another 2 minutes until all ingredients are combined and dough forms. Wrap dough in plastic wrap and refrigerate for 1 hour.

3. Preheat oven to 350°F. Working on a well-floured surface, roll out dough to a thickness of about ⅛ inch. Using a star-shaped cookie cutter, cut stars out of the dough. Bake for 10-12 minutes until golden and crisp. Allow to cool completely on a cooling rack before decorating.

4. *Make the frosting:* In a medium bowl, mix together the powdered sugar, corn syrup and lemon juice until the mixture is smooth and has a paste-like texture. Divide the frosting into three separate bowls. Add a few drops of red food coloring in one bowl until the desired color is achieved. Do the same with the second bowl by adding a few drops of blue food coloring. The frosting in the third bowl should remain white.

5. *Decorate the cookies:* Spread 1 heaped tablespoon of frosting onto each cookie and use a small offset spatula or the back end of knife to smooth out frosting. Sprinkle colored sugar onto frosting and allow it to harden before serving. Cookies can be stored in an airtight container at room temperature for up to 3 days.

Valentine's Day Cookies

The best part about these cookies is their frosting. Grab your valentine and decorate these together for a more meaningful dessert.

Ingredients

3 cups all-purpose flour

¾ cup powdered sugar

1½ sticks (6 oz.) butter

1 teaspoon baking powder

2 egg yolks

½ cup heavy cream

1 tablespoon pure vanilla extract

For frosting

2 egg whites, at room temperature

¼ teaspoon cream of tartar

4 cups powdered sugar

Red food coloring

½ cup colored sugar (pink or red)

Preparation

1. Using a mixer fitted with a paddle attachment, mix together the flour, powdered sugar, butter and baking powder on medium speed until the mixture has a crumb-like consistency. Add the egg yolks, heavy cream and vanilla extract, and mix for 1 minute until dough is formed. Wrap the dough in plastic wrap and refrigerate for 1 hour.

2. Preheat oven to 350°F. Working on a well-floured surface, roll out dough to a thickness of about ⅛ inch. Using a heart-shaped cookie cutter, cut hearts out of the dough.

3. Bake for 18-20 minutes until golden and crisp. Allow to cool completely on a cooling rack before decorating.

4. *Make the frosting:* Using a mixer fitted with a whisk attachment, mix together the egg whites and cream of tartar on medium speed for 2 minutes until a lightly whipped cream is formed. Add the powdered sugar and continue to whisk for another 2 minutes until stiff, glossy peaks form. Add a few drops of red or pink food coloring until the desired color is achieved.

5. *Decorate the cookies:* Spread 1 heaped tablespoon of frosting onto each cookie and use a small offset spatula or the back end of knife to smooth out frosting. Sprinkle colored sugar onto frosting and allow it to harden before serving.

6. Cookies can be stored in an airtight container at room temperature for up to 3 days.

MAKES **45** COOKIES

Hamantaschens

These triangle-shaped cookies,
traditionally eaten on the Jewish
holiday Purim, can be adapted with
different fillings, including
chocolate or fruit jam.

Ingredients

1¾ sticks (7 oz.) butter, at room temperature

⅓ cup sugar

1 egg + 1 egg, beaten

2½ cups all-purpose flour

¼ cup orange juice

For poppy filling

7 oz. ground poppy seeds

2 cups sugar

½ stick (2 oz.) butter

¼ cup orange juice

½ cup graham crackers, crumbled

For decoration

½ cup powdered sugar

Preparation

1. Using a mixer fitted with a whisk attachment, mix together the butter and sugar on medium speed for 2 minutes until light and fluffy. Add one egg and continue mixing until the mixture is creamy.

2. Reduce mixer speed to low and alternatively add the flour and orange juice. Once all ingredients are combined and dough is formed, wrap in plastic wrap and refrigerate for 1 hour.

3. ***Make the poppy seed filling:*** In a small saucepan, heat the ground poppy seeds, sugar, butter and orange juice on medium heat. Stir continuously for 10 minutes until the mixture is smooth. Add the graham crackers, remove from heat and allow mixture to chill to room temperature.

4. Preheat oven to 350°F. Working on a well-floured surface, roll out dough to a thickness of about ⅛ inch. Using a 3-inch round cookie cutter, cut circles out of the dough.

5. Beat the remaining egg and brush the edges of one circle. Drop 1 teaspoon of the poppy filling in the center of the circle and fold in the sides to form a triangle. Pinch dough together in the middle to enclose the filling. Brush the outside edges with egg. Repeat with the remaining circles.

6. Bake for 18-20 minutes until golden. Allow to cool on a cooling rack before serving. Dust evenly with powdered sugar before serving.

7. Cookies may be stored in an airtight container at room temperature for up to 3 days.

MAKES **30** COOKIES

Cookies for the Health Conscious

Energy Bars

An important ingredient in these energy bars is flax seeds. They not only contain high levels of dietary fiber and omega-3 fatty acids, but are also super tasty.

Ingredients

¾ stick (3 oz.) butter

½ cup honey

¼ teaspoon salt

1 teaspoon ground cinnamon

1 cup dark brown sugar, packed

1½ cups old-fashioned rolled oats

⅓ cup sunflower seeds

¼ cup flax seeds

⅓ cup dried figs, finely chopped

⅓ cup raisins

¼ cup dried apricots, finely chopped

¼ cup whole wheat flour

Preparation

1. In a medium saucepan, heat the butter, honey, salt, cinnamon and brown sugar on low heat for 5 minutes, until all ingredients are combined.

2. Remove from heat and allow mixture to cool to room temperature. Add the rolled oats, sunflower seeds, flax seeds, dried figs, raisins and apricots to the pan and stir until combined. Gradually add the flour, while stirring constantly until combined. The mixture should be thick and sticky.

3. Preheat oven to 340°F. Pour mixture into non-stick, rectangular, 2-inch silicon financier mold. Bake for 13-15 minutes. Allow to cool completely on a cooling rack before removing from mold.

4. Cookies can be stored in an airtight container at room temperature for up to 1 week.

MAKES 40 BARS

Tehini & Agave Cookies

Agave syrup is a natural sweetener derived from the agave plant, which is found mainly in Mexico. The syrup can be bought from health-food markets, or can be replaced with honey for this recipe. These cookies have a very crumbly consistency, so make sure to let them cool completely before serving.

Ingredients

1¾ sticks (7 oz.) butter, at room temperature
½ cup sugar
½ cup agave syrup
1 cup raw tehini
3 cups all-purpose flour
¼ teaspoon salt
2 tablespoons baking powder

Preparation

1. Using a mixer fitted with a paddle attachment, mix together the butter, sugar and agave syrup on medium speed for 2 minutes. Add the tehini and continue mixing. Gradually add the flour, salt and baking powder until all ingredients are combined well.

2. Preheat oven to 350°F. Wet your hands slightly, scoop out a small ping pong-sized ball of dough, and place on a baking sheet lined with parchment paper. Repeat with the remaining dough, spacing the cookies 2 inches apart. Use the back of a fork to make an indentation in the center of each cookie.

3. Bake for 10-12 minutes until golden. Allow to cool completely on a cooling rack before serving.

4. Cookies may be stored in an airtight container at room temperature for up to a week.

MAKES 40 COOKIES

Ginger & Molasses Cookies

Ginger is known to provide
a plethora of health benefits.
For this recipe, simply peel
the outer layer of skin off
and grate the ginger, using a small
or microplane grater.

Ingredients

1½ cups all-purpose flour

¼ teaspoon salt

½ teaspoon baking soda

1 stick (4 oz.) butter, at room temperature

½ cup light brown sugar

1 egg

¾ cup molasses

1 tablespoon pure vanilla extract

1 teaspoon fresh ginger, finely grated

Preparation

1. In a large bowl, sift together flour, salt and baking soda.

2. Using a mixer fitted with a whisk attachment, mix together the butter and brown sugar on medium speed for 2 minutes, until creamy. Add the egg, molasses, vanilla extract and ginger. Continue mixing for another 3 minutes, until all ingredients are combined.

3. Reduce mixer speed to low. Gradually add the dry ingredients and continue mixing for another 2 minutes, until all ingredients are combined and dough forms. Wrap dough in plastic wrap and refrigerate for 1 hour.

4. Preheat oven to 340°F. Wet your hands slightly and roll the dough into 1½-inch balls and place onto baking sheets lined with parchment paper, spacing about 2 inches apart.

5. Bake for 12-15 minutes until hardened. Transfer to a cooling rack to cool completely before serving.

6. Cookies may be stored in an airtight container at room temperature for up to 1 week.

MAKES 30 COOKIES

Macadamia & Molasses Cookies

MAKES **60** COOKIES

Of all known nuts, macadamia nuts have the highest amount of beneficial monosaturated fats. They are highly nutritious, making these cookies are great choice for a healthy snack.

Ingredients

1½ cups all-purpose flour

¾ cup whole wheat flour

¼ teaspoon salt

1 teaspoon baking powder

1 teaspoon ground cinnamon

½ teaspoon ground nutmeg

¾ stick (3 oz.) butter

½ cup sugar

¼ cup molasses

1 egg

1 teaspoon lemon zest

3.5 oz. macadamia nuts, chopped
+ 7 oz. whole macadamia nuts for decoration

Preparation

1. In a large bowl, sift together both flours, salt, baking powder, cinnamon and nutmeg.

2. Using a stand mixer fitted with a whisk attachment, mix together the butter, sugar and molasses on medium speed for 2 minutes. Add the egg and continue mixing until combined.

3. Gradually add the dry ingredients to the mixer and continue whisking until combined well. Add the lemon zest and chopped macadamia nuts, and mix for 1 minute.

4. Preheat oven to 350°F. Using a 1½-inch ice cream scoop, drop dough onto baking sheets lined with parchment paper, spacing about 2 inches apart. Gently press one whole macadamia nut into the center of each cookie.

5. Bake for 10-12 minutes, until crisp on the outside and soft on the inside. Allow to cool completely on a cooling rack before serving.

6. Cookies may be stored in an airtight container at room temperature for up to 1 week.

Sesame Bars

Sesame seeds are remarkably
rich in iron, magnesium,
manganese, copper, and calcium.
Make sure your sesame seeds
are fresh by tasting one;
if it has a bitter taste, then
the seeds have gone bad.

Ingredients

1 lbs. 5 oz. toasted sesame seeds
1½ cups sugar
1 cup canola oil
3 eggs
½ cup self-raising flour

Preparation

1. Preheat oven to 340°F. In a large bowl, mix all ingredients together until combined well.

2. Pour the mixture onto a baking pan lined with parchment paper and use a spatula to spread it out so that it is about ¾ inch in height.

3. Bake for 12-15 minutes until hardened. Allow to cool completely on a cooling rack.

4. Once completely cooled, use a sharp knife to cut out 1-inch x 2-inch rectangles. Bars can be stored in an airtight container at room temperature for up to 1 week.

MAKES
30
BARS

Cranberry Oatmeal Cookies

These healthy cookies stay soft and warm in the center, making them a great treat on a winter morning.

Ingredients

1⅓ cups whole wheat flour

⅓ cup all-purpose flour

1 teaspoon ground cinnamon

¼ teaspoon salt

1 teaspoon baking powder

1¾ sticks (7 oz.) butter, at room temperature

¾ cup brown sugar

1 egg

1½ cups old-fashioned rolled oats

1 cup dried cranberries

Preparation

1. In a large bowl, sift together both flours, cinnamon, salt, and baking powder.

2. Using a mixer fitted with a paddle attachment, mix together the butter and brown sugar on medium speed for 2 minutes, until the mixture is light and fluffy. Add the egg and continue mixing.

3. Reduce mixer speed to low and gradually add the dry mixture, rolled oats and cranberries. Continue mixing until all ingredients are incorporated and dough forms. Wrap dough in plastic wrap and refrigerate for 2 hours.

4. Preheat oven to 350°F. Wet your hands slightly and roll the dough into 1½-inch balls. Place them onto baking sheets lined with parchment paper, spacing about 2 inches apart.

5. Bake for 12-15 minutes until golden. Transfer to a cooling rack to cool completely before serving.

6. Cookies may be stored in an airtight container at room temperature for up to 1 week.

MAKES 30 COOKIES

Green Tea Cookies

Brazil nuts are a great source of magnesium and thiamine, while green tea has been shown to lower chances of heart disease and of developing certain types of cancer. Together, these two ingredients help to make up one super nutritious cookie.

Ingredients

1 cup whole wheat flour

1 cup all-purpose flour

¼ teaspoon salt

1 tablespoon baking powder

½ teaspoon baking soda

1 cup old-fashioned rolled oats

¾ cup light brown sugar

⅓ cup canola oil

½ cup soy milk

½ cup green tea (made from ½ cup hot water + 1 green tea bag)

½ cup brazil nuts, coarsely chopped

Preparation

1. Preheat oven to 350°F. In a large bowl, mix together both flours, salt, baking powder, baking soda and rolled oats.

2. In a separate bowl, mix together the sugar, oil, soy milk and green tea. Gradually add the dry ingredients and brazil nuts, and mix until all ingredients are combined. Cover bowl with plastic wrap and refrigerate for 1 hour.

3. Wet your hands slightly and roll the dough into 1½-inch balls and place onto baking sheets lined with parchment paper, spacing about 2 inches apart.

4. Bake for 20-22 minutes until hardened. Transfer to a cooling rack to cool completely before serving.

5. Cookies may be stored in an airtight container at room temperature for up to 1 week.

MAKES 35 COOKIES

Granola Cookies

MAKES **35** COOKIES

Granola, served with yogurt
and fresh fruit, is no doubt one
of my favorite breakfasts.
When I don't have time for
a sit-down breakfast, these cookies
are a great, healthy, and filling
replacement.

Ingredients

¾ cup all-purpose flour

1 teaspoon baking powder

1 teaspoon ground ginger

½ teaspoon ground cloves

¾ stick (3 oz.) butter, at room temperature

½ cup brown sugar

1 egg

1 cup toasted granola

⅓ cup light raisins

¼ cup sunflower seeds

¼ cup pumpkin seeds

¼ cup almond slivers

Preparation

1. In a large bowl, sift together the flour, baking powder, ginger and cloves.

2. Using a mixer fitted with a paddle attachment, mix together the butter and brown sugar on medium speed for 2 minutes, until the mixture is light and fluffy. Add the egg and continue mixing.

3. Reduce mixer speed to low and gradually add the dry ingredients, granola, raisins, sunflower seeds, pumpkin seeds and almond slivers. Continue mixing until all ingredients are combined and dough forms. Wrap dough in plastic wrap and refrigerate for 2 hours.

4. Preheat oven to 350°F. Wet your hands slightly and roll the dough into 1½-inch balls and place onto baking sheets lined with parchment paper, spacing about 2 inches apart.

5. Bake for 12-15 minutes until golden. Transfer to a cooling rack to cool completely before serving.

6. Cookies may be stored in an airtight container at room temperature for up to 1 week.

Semolina & Almond Cookies

MAKES **20** COOKIES

Instead of using butter, these cookies are made with canola oil, which has a beneficial omega-3 fatty acid profile. Don't be alarmed if the dough comes out a bit oily—the cookies will come out perfectly crisp.

Ingredients

⅓ cup semolina

1 cup powdered sugar

2 cups all-purpose flour

1 tablespoon baking powder

1 tablespoon lemon zest

2 teaspoons cinnamon

½ teaspoon ground cloves

½ teaspoon ground ginger

1 egg

¾ cup canola oil

20 whole blanched almonds

For the syrup

1 cup sugar

1 cup water

¼ cup honey

Preparation

1. In a large bowl, mix together all ingredients except for the egg, oil and almonds.

2. Add the egg and mix. Gradually add the oil and mix, until all ingredients are combined.

3. Preheat oven to 340°F. Using a 1½-inch ice cream scoop, drop dough onto baking sheets lined with parchment paper, spacing about 2 inches apart. Gently press one almond into the center of each cookie.

4. Bake cookies for 12-15 minutes.

5. *Make the syrup:* Place all ingredients in a small saucepan on low heat and cook for 12 minutes, until the sugar has dissolved and the mixture has thickened. Dip each cookie into the syrup as soon as it comes out of the oven and still hot.

6. Allow to cool completely on a cooling rack before serving.

7. Cookies may be stored in an airtight container at room temperature for up to 1 week.

Pine Nut Cookies

Pine nuts are a great source of dietary fiber. They come in a variety of sizes, depending on the species. I prefer to use the smaller ones for these delicious cookies.

Ingredients

2 cups all-purpose flour

¾ cup cornmeal

1½ sticks (6 oz.) butter, cubed

¼ teaspoon salt

1 cup + ¼ cup powdered sugar

2 egg yolks + 1 egg, beaten

2 cups pine nuts

Preparation

1. Using a mixer fitted with a paddle attachment, mix together the flour, cornmeal, butter, salt and 1 cup of powdered sugar on medium speed for 2 minutes, until the mixture has a crumb-like texture. Add the egg yolks and mix for 1 minute until dough is formed. Wrap dough in plastic wrap and refrigerate for 1 hour.

2. Preheat oven to 340°F. Wet your hands slightly and roll the dough into 1½-inch balls, brush with beaten egg and roll in pine nuts, pressing the pine nuts slightly into the cookies with your fingers. Brush again with beaten egg and place onto baking sheets lined with parchment paper, spacing about 2 inches apart

3. Bake for 15-18 minutes until golden brown. Transfer to a cooling rack to cool completely. Sprinkle with the remaining powdered sugar and serve.

4. Cookies may be stored in an airtight container at room temperature for up to 1 week.

MAKES 32 COOKIES

Sugar-Free Lemon Cookies

You can use any sugar substitute of your choice here; just be aware that some are sweeter than others and may change the sweetness of the cookie.

Ingredients

1¼ cups all-purpose flour

1¾ sticks (7 oz.) butter,
cold and cut into cubes

¼ teaspoon salt

½ cup sugar substitute

4 tablespoons fresh lemon juice

1 egg

1 tablespoon lemon zest

Preparation

1. Using a mixer fitted with a paddle attachment, mix together the flour, butter, salt, and sugar substitute on medium speed for 3 minutes until the mixture has a crumb-like texture. Add the lemon juice, egg and lemon zest, and mix for 1 minute until dough is formed. Wrap the dough in plastic wrap and refrigerate for 1 hour.

2. Preheat oven to 320°F. Wet your hands slightly and roll the dough into 1½-inch balls and place onto baking sheets lined with parchment paper, spacing about 2 inches apart. Firmly press fork tines into each dough ball, making a pattern.

3. Bake for 15-18 minutes. Transfer to a cooling rack to cool completely before serving.

4. Cookies may be stored in an airtight container at room temperature for up to 1 week.

MAKES 30 COOKIES

Pistachio & Cardamom Cookies

Native to India, cardamom has a strong, unique taste and an intensely aromatic fragrance that gives these cookies their unique flavor.

Ingredients

1 cup whole wheat flour

1¼ cups all-purpose flour

1 tablespoon ground cardamom

½ teaspoon ground cloves

¼ teaspoon salt

1 teaspoon baking powder

2 sticks (8 oz.) butter, at room temperature

½ cup brown sugar

2 eggs

1 tablespoon almond extract

5 oz. raw shelled pistachios, coarsely chopped

Preparation

1. In a large bowl, sift together both flours, ground cardamom, ground cloves, salt and baking powder.

2. Using a mixer fitted with a paddle attachment, mix together the butter and brown sugar on medium speed for 2 minutes, until light and fluffy. Gradually add the eggs, one at a time, and then add the almond extract and continue mixing.

3. Reduce mixer speed to low and gradually add the dry ingredients. Add the chopped pistachios, and mix for 1 minute until all ingredients are combined.

4. Divide the dough into two equal parts. Roll ½ of the dough into a 1-inch diameter log and wrap with plastic wrap. Repeat with the second ½ of dough. Place the dough logs on a sheet of parchment paper and place in the freezer for 30 minutes, until the dough has hardened.

5. Preheat oven to 350°F. Remove the dough from the freezer and using a sharp knife, cut the dough into ½-inch slices and place on a baking sheet, spacing 1 inch apart.

6. Bake for 18-20 minutes, until pale gold in color. Cool on sheet on a cooling rack.

7. Cookies can be stored in an airtight container at room temperature for up to 1 week.

MAKES 60 COOKIES

Cookies for Chocolate Lovers

Triple Chocolate Chip Cookies

Your much-loved chocolate chip
has been upgraded
to the most chocolatey chip
you've ever tasted!

Ingredients

½ cup all-purpose flour
1 tablespoon baking powder
¼ teaspoon salt
1¼ sticks (5 oz.) butter, at room temperature
1 cup sugar
1 egg
⅔ cup dark chocolate chips
⅔ cup milk chocolate chips
⅔ cup white chocolate chips

Preparation

1. In a large bowl, sift together the flour, baking powder and salt.

2. Using a mixer fitted with a whisk attachment, mix together the butter and sugar for 2 minutes on medium speed, until light and fluffy. Add the egg and continue whisking until combined.

3. Reduce mixer speed to low, gradually add the dry ingredients, and continue to mix for 3 minutes, until all ingredients are combined and dough forms.

4. Use a spoon or flexible spatula to mix in the chocolate chips.

5. Preheat oven to 350°F. Wet your hands slightly and roll the dough into 1½-inch balls and place onto baking sheets lined with parchment paper, spacing about 2 inches apart.

6. Bake for 12-15 minutes. Transfer to a cooling rack to cool completely before serving.

7. Cookies may be stored in an airtight container at room temperature for up to 1 week.

MAKES 50 COOKIES

Brownies

Is there really anything better
than a warm brownie
to warm the heart?

Ingredients

3 cups all-purpose flour
1¾ cups sugar
¼ teaspoon salt
1 teaspoon baking soda
10.5 oz. dark chocolate
2½ sticks (10 oz.) butter
5 eggs
2 tablespoons pure vanilla extract
For baking
One 12-inch x 14-inch baking dish

Preparation

1. In a large bowl, sift together the flour, sugar, salt and baking soda. Melt chocolate and butter in a heatproof bowl, set over a pan of simmering water. Stir occasionally. Remove from heat and allow mixture to cool to room temperature. Add the eggs, one at a time, then add the vanilla extract and mix until mixture is smooth.

2. Gradually add the dry ingredients to the chocolate mixture and mix until all ingredients are combined.

3. Preheat oven to 350°F and line a 12-inch x 14-inch baking dish with parchment paper.

4. Pour batter evenly into baking dish and bake for 25-30 minutes until a toothpick, inserted in the center, comes out dry.

5. Allow to chill to room temperature before cutting into 2-inch squares.

6. Cookies may be stored in an airtight container at room temperature for up to 1 week.

MAKES **30** BROWNIES

Blondies

The brownies' cousin - the blondie - is just as rich, but has a velvety caramel and maple flavor.

Ingredients

2 cups all-purpose flour
¼ teaspoon salt
1 teaspoon baking powder
1¾ sticks (7 oz.) butter, at room temperature
1 cup light brown sugar
⅔ cup maple syrup
1 tablespoon pure vanilla extract
3 eggs
¾ cup white chocolate chips

For baking

One 12-inch x 14-inch baking dish

Preparation

1. In a large bowl, sift together the flour, salt and baking powder.

2. In a separate bowl, whisk together the butter and brown sugar, and then add the maple syrup and vanilla extract. Continue to whisk until mixture is smooth. Add the eggs, one at a time, and mix until combined.

3. Gradually add the dry ingredients to the mixture and whisk until the mixture is combined well. Add the white chocolate chips and mix.

4. Preheat oven to 350°F and line a 12-inch x 14-inch baking dish with parchment paper.

5. Pour batter evenly into baking dish and bake for 25-30 minutes until golden and a toothpick, inserted in the center, comes out dry.

6. Allow to chill to room temperature before cutting into 2-inch squares.

7. Cookies may be stored in an airtight container at room temperature for up to 1 week.

MAKES 30 BLONDIES

Chocolate Ganache Cookie Sandwich

Ganache is a glaze made by mixing chocolate and heavy cream. Spread it between two chocolate cookies for the perfect chocolate sandwich.

Ingredients

¾ cup all-purpose flour
¾ cup cocoa powder
½ tablespoon baking powder
¼ teaspoon baking soda
¼ teaspoon salt
1¾ sticks (7 oz.) butter, at room temperature
1 cup sugar
2 eggs
For the chocolate ganache filling
¾ cup heavy cream
1⅓ cups dark chocolate, coarsely chopped
½ stick (2 oz.) butter, at room temperature

Preparation

1. In a large bowl, sift together the flour, cocoa powder, baking powder, baking soda and salt.

2. Using a mixer fitted with a whisk attachment, mix together the butter and sugar on medium speed for 3 minutes, until light and fluffy. Add the eggs, one at a time, and continue to mix until mixture is smooth.

3. Reduce mixer speed to low and gradually add dry ingredients. Mix for 1-2 minutes until all ingredients are combined. Cover bowl with plastic wrap and refrigerate for 2 hours.

4. Preheat oven to 350°F. Wet your hands slightly and roll the dough into 1½-inch balls. Place onto baking sheets lined with parchment paper, spacing about 2 inches apart. Gently press each cookie to flatten slightly.

5. Bake for 12-15 minutes. Transfer to a cooling rack to cool completely. Prepare the ganache: In a small saucepan, heat the heavy cream on low heat until just barely simmering. Remove from heat, add the chocolate, and stir until the chocolate has completely melted. Allow to chill for 5 minutes, add butter, and stir until combined. Refrigerate ganache for 30 minutes.

6. Make the sandwiches: Place a heaped teaspoon of ganache on the smooth side of one cookie and close the sandwich with a second cookie. Cookies can be kept in an airtight container in the refrigerator for up to 1 week.

MAKES **30** COOKIE SANDWICHES

Chocolate Truffles

It's very important to follow the instructions for this recipe to a tee. If not, you may end up with scrambled eggs! Once you've completed all the steps, you can place the mixture in the freezer to speed up the cooling process.

Ingredients

2¾ sticks (7 oz.) butter

2 cups heavy cream

8 egg yolks

½ cup sugar

1¾ pounds dark chocolate, broken up into cubes

14 oz. milk chocolate, broken up into cubes

¼ cup brandy

2½ cups cocoa powder, for coating

Preparation

1. In a medium saucepan, heat the butter and heavy cream, just until bubbles appear on the edges, making sure not to let the mixture come to a complete boil. Remove from heat.

2. In a separate bowl, whisk together the egg yolks and sugar for about 3 minutes.

3. In batches, gradually add the butter and heavy cream mixture to the eggs and stir constantly.

4. Return the entire mixture to the saucepan and cook on low heat while constantly stirring for several minutes, until the mixture has thickened to a creamy consistency. Remove from heat, add the dark chocolate and milk chocolate to the mixture, and allow it to stand for 2 minutes.

5. Using a whisk, beginning at the center of the saucepan, start mixing until smooth. Add the brandy and whisk for 1 minute. Transfer mixture to a clean bowl, cover with plastic wrap and refrigerate for at least 2 hours, until the mixture is completely cold.

6. Using a spoon that has been immersed in hot water, scoop out a golf-sized ball of the mixture and immediate roll each ball in cocoa powder.

7. Truffles must be kept in an airtight container in the refrigerator for up to 2 weeks.

∼ Playing around ∼

To make square-shaped truffles, pour the warm mixture onto a baking sheet lined with parchment paper, and refrigerate it. Once the mixture is completely cold, use a sharp knife to cut it into squares and then roll each square in cocoa powder.

MAKES 80 TRUFFLES

Chocolate & Caramel Fudge Squares

These chocolate and caramel fudge squares will remind you of your favorite candy bar, but will be even better because they are homemade!

Ingredients

¾ cup heavy cream

⅓ cup whole milk

⅔ cup sugar

2½ tablespoons glucose or light corn syrup

1 tablespoon pure vanilla extract

¾ sticks (3 oz.) salted butter, cut into cubes

⅔ cup dark chocolate, cut into cubes

½ cup whole shelled pistachios

1 cup whole hazelnuts

For baking

One 7-inch square baking dish, lined with a silicon baking sheet or parchment paper

Baking thermometer

Preparation

1. In a medium saucepan, heat the heavy cream, milk, sugar, corn syrup, vanilla extract and butter. Stir constantly over low heat until the mixture reaches 235°F.

2. Remove from heat and add chocolate, pistachios and hazelnuts. Mix until all ingredients are combined.

3. Pour the mixture into the lined baking dish and allow it to cool to room temperature. Once completely cool, use a sharp knife to cut out 1-inch squares.

4. Cookies can be stored in the refrigerator in an airtight container for up to two weeks, or in the freezer for up to 2 months.

MAKES 50 SQUARES

Chocolate Crackles

These cracked cookies are covered with nooks and crannies, providing the perfect amount of space for the powdered sugar to rest in. If you are in a rush, you can place the batter in the freezer for 1 hour, instead of for 3 hours in the fridge.

Ingredients

3 eggs
1 cup sugar
¾ pound (12 oz.) dark chocolate
½ stick (2 oz.) butter
2 cups all-purpose flour
¼ teaspoon salt
1 teaspoon baking powder
2 tablespoons brandy
For decoration
2¼ cups powdered sugar

Preparation

1. Using a mixer fitted with a whisk attachment, mix the eggs and sugar until the mixture is light and fluffy.

2. Melt chocolate in a heatproof bowl, set over a pan of simmering water. Stir occasionally. Add the butter and stir until butter is incorporated. Remove from heat and allow mixture to cool to room temperature.

3. Add the melted chocolate to the egg mixture and mix until smooth.

4. Add the flour, salt, and baking powder and fold the mixture until all ingredients are combined well. Add the brandy and continue to fold. Place the batter in the refrigerator for 3 hours until firm.

5. Preheat oven to 350°F. Using a 1½-inch ice cream scoop, make balls out of dough and roll each one in powdered sugar to coat them. Place balls on baking sheets lined with parchment paper, spacing about 2 inches apart.

6. Bake for 10-12 minutes, until surfaces crack. Allow cookies to cool on a cooling rack before serving.

7. Cookies may be stored in an airtight container at room temperature for up to 3 days.

MAKES **50** COOKIES

Chocolate Coffee Tuiles

Tuile, pronounced "tweel",
is the French word for tile.
These cookies have intricate
detailing, which some might say
is similar to tile.

Ingredients

¼ cup milk
¾ stick (3 oz.) butter, melted
1¾ cups powdered sugar
⅔ cup all-purpose flour
¼ cup cocoa powder
2 tablespoons instant coffee powder

Preparation

1. In a large bowl, whisk together the milk and butter and gradually add the powdered sugar, flour, cocoa powder and coffee. Whisk until all ingredients are combined. Cover the bowl with plastic wrap and refrigerate for at least 3 hours.

2. Preheat oven to 340°F. Pour the batter onto a silicon baking sheet and using an offset spatula spread the batter thinly until a thin, even layer is formed.

3. Bake for 8-10 minutes until crispy. Allow it to stand for 5 minutes, until completely cool, and then break the tuiles into pieces.

4. Cookies may be stored in an airtight container at room temperature for up to 2 days.

MAKES 75 COOKIES

Orange Chocolate Fudge Cookies

True chocolate lovers know that chocolate and orange are a divine combination, which makes these cookies heavenly.

Ingredients

3 cups dark chocolate, coarsely chopped
⅔ cup milk chocolate, coarsely chopped
¾ stick (3 oz.) butter, at room temperature
2 tablespoons orange zest
⅔ cups all-purpose flour
½ teaspoon baking powder
¼ teaspoon salt
4 eggs + 1 egg yolk
1 cup sugar

Preparation

1. Place dark chocolate, milk chocolate, butter and orange zest in a heatproof bowl, set over a pan of simmering water, and stir until ingredients have melted. Remove from heat and allow mixture to cool to room temperature.

2. In a separate bowl, sift together the flour, baking powder and salt.

3. Using a mixer fitted with a whisk attachment, whisk together the eggs, egg yolk and sugar for 5 minutes on medium speed, until light and fluffy. Add the melted chocolate to the mixer and continue whisking.

4. Reduce mixer speed to low and gradually add the dry ingredients.

5. Continue mixing for another 2-3 minutes, until all ingredients are combined. Cover bowl with plastic wrap and refrigerate for 30 minutes.

6. Preheat oven to 350°F. Using a 1½-inch ice cream scoop, drop dough onto baking sheets lined with parchment paper, spacing about 1½ inches apart.

7. Bake for 10-12 minutes until hardened. Transfer to a cooling rack to cool completely before serving.

8. Cookies may be stored in an airtight container at room temperature for up to 1 week.

MAKES 50 COOKIES

White Chocolate Cinnamon Lollipops

You don't have to use a silicon mold if you don't have one. Simply make small balls using your hands, but make sure to coat your hands first with powdered sugar so that the chocolate doesn't stick. Roll balls in crushed pistachios before freezing. Freeze on a baking sheet lined with parchment paper.

Ingredients

¾ cup heavy cream

¾ stick (3 oz.) butter

4 egg yolks

½ cup sugar

4 cups white chocolate, coarsely chopped

2 tablespoons brandy

20 cinnamon sticks (or popsicle sticks)

For decoration

1 cup finely crushed pistachios

For baking

1 silicon baking sheet with 1½ inch round molds

Preparation

1. In a medium saucepan, combine the heavy cream and butter and cook on low heat for around 5 minutes, until the butter has melted and the mixture is combined.

2. Using a mixer fitted with a whisk attachment, whisk the egg yolks and sugar for 2 minutes. Add a small amount of the heavy cream mixture to the mixer (to temper) and then gradually add the rest of the heavy cream to the eggs.

3. Return the mixture to the saucepan and cook on low heat, stirring constantly for about 3-4 minutes, until thickened. Remove from heat.

4. Place the white chocolate in a large bowl and pour the thickened cream over the chocolate. Stir until the mixture is smooth. Add the brandy and continue mixing until all ingredients are combined.

5. Place 1 teaspoon of the crushed pistachios in the bottom of each mold.

6. Pour mixture into the silicon mold (on top of pistachios) and freeze for about 40 minutes until mixture just begins to harden. Place a cinnamon stick halfway in each mold and return to freezer for at least 1 hour, until completely hardened.

7. Cookies can be stored in the refrigerator in an airtight container for up to 3 weeks.

MAKES **30** LOLLIPOPS

Mendiants

A mendiant is a traditional french cookie, consisting of a chocolate disk adorned with nuts and dried fruits. These represent the four mendiant or monastic orders of the Dominicans, Augustinian, Franciscans and Carmelites. This recipe calls for a baking thermometer, which can be found in professional baking stores.

Ingredients

3 cups dark chocolate, coarsely chopped (preferably above 60% cocoa)

¾ cup hazelnuts

½ cup walnuts

⅓ cup yellow raisins

¾ cup pistachios

⅓ cup almond slivers

¼ cup dried cranberries

¼ cup dried apricots, coarsely chopped

For baking

Baking thermometer

Preparation

1. Melt chocolate in a heatproof bowl, set over a pan of simmering water. Stir occasionally until chocolate reaches 104-113°F. Remove from heat and refrigerate until the chocolate cools to 75-78°F. Return chocolate to heat until it reaches 86-89°F.

2. Pour chocolate evenly onto a baking sheet lined to parchment paper and smooth out to a height of about ⅓ inch. Mix remaining ingredients in a bowl and then pour evenly onto the chocolate, gently pressing them into the chocolate.

3. Refrigerate for 15 minutes. Using a 2-inch cookie cutter, cut out circles.

4. Cookies may be kept in an airtight container in the refrigerator for up to 1 week.

Cookies for the Connoisseur

Raspberry Macaroons

MAKES **60** MACAROONS

Although many debate the origins of macaroons, they are believed to have been created in 791 A.D. in a convent near Cormery, France. Widely sold in bakeries all over France, there is even a museum of this cookie in the french city of Montmorillon.

Ingredients

2½ + 2 cups powdered sugar

2½ cups, ground almonds

5 egg whites, at room temperature

½ cup sugar

Pink food coloring

4 tablespoons cold water

For the raspberry cream

3.5 oz. fresh raspberries
(or frozen, defrosted and drained)

½ cup powdered sugar

½ tablespoon fresh lemon juice

5 egg yolks

2½ tablespoons cornstarch

½ cup sugar

1 cup heavy cream

Preparation

1. Using a fine sieve, sift together 2½ cups of the powdered sugar and ground almonds.

2. Using a mixer fitted with a whisk attachment, whisk the egg whites at medium speed for 8 minutes. Gradually add the sugar and the rest of the powdered sugar, as well as about 5 drops of food coloring.

3. Using a flexible rubber spatula, fold the mixture of powdered sugar and ground almonds carefully into the beaten egg whites. As soon as the mixture becomes smooth and there are no streaks of egg white, stop folding and scrape the batter into a pastry bag.

4. Pipe the batter onto a baking sheet lined with parchment paper in 1-inch circles (about 1 tablespoon of batter each), spacing the cookies 1 inch apart.

5. Preheat oven to 320°F. Allow baking sheet to stand at room temperature for 30 minutes, so that the outside layer of the macaroons hardens slightly.

6. Bake for 12-15 minutes. Once the baking sheet is removed from oven, pour 4 tablespoons of cold water onto the parchment paper. This will stop the macaroons from overcooking and will make it easier to remove them once they have cooled completely.

7. *Make raspberry cream:* Mix the raspberries, powdered sugar and lemon juice in a food processor until smooth, and then use a fine sieve to strain the mixture.

8. In a large bowl, whisk together the egg yolks, cornstarch and sugar with 2 tablespoons of the heavy cream.

9. In a small saucepan, heat the remaining heavy cream on low heat until just barely simmering. Remove from heat and whisk a few tablespoons of the cream into the yolk mixture. Gradually add the remaining cream, whisking constantly.

10. Return mixture to saucepan and heat on low heat, while stirring constantly for 5-8 minutes until a thick cream is formed. Remove from heat and cool to room temperature. Add the raspberry mixture and mix until smooth. Refrigerate for 2 hours until cream has thickened.

11. *Assemble the macaroons:* Place filling into a pastry bag fitted with a round tip and pipe filling onto half of the smooth side of the macaroons and close each sandwich with a second macaron.

12. Cookies may be stored in an airtight container in the refrigerator for up to 1 week.

Espresso Cookies

If you love to drink a good espresso in the morning, these cookies will be the perfect complement.

Ingredients

2 cups all-purpose flour

2 tablespoons cocoa powder

¼ teaspoon salt

1 tablespoon baking powder

1 teaspoon finely-ground, dark-roast coffee

4 tablespoons boiling water

1¼ sticks (6 oz.) butter, at room temperature

1 cup dark brown sugar, packed

1 egg yolk

For decoration

1 egg, beaten

1 tablespoon water

⅓ cup demerara sugar

⅓ cup cocoa powder (optional)

Preparation

1. In a large bowl, sift together the flour, cocoa powder, salt and baking powder.

2. In a small bowl, mix together the ground coffee and boiling water. Allow to cool to room temperature.

3. Using a mixer fitted with a paddle attachment, mix together the butter and brown sugar on medium speed for 3 minutes, until light and fluffy. Add the egg yolk and the coffee mixture and continue to mix until combined.

4. Reduce mixer speed to low and gradually add the dry ingredients. Continue to mix until all ingredients are combined and dough forms. Divide the dough into two equal parts. Roll each half into a 1-inch diameter log. (If the dough is too soft, you can refrigerate it for 15 minutes before rolling out.)

5. Place the dough log on a sheet of parchment paper and place in the freezer for about 15 minutes, until the dough has hardened.

6. Preheat oven to 320°F. Combine the egg and water to make an egg wash. Remove the dough from the freezer and brush with the egg wash. Roll the dough in the sugar and cocoa powder, making sure that they stick to the dough and that the dough is generously covered in sugar (some will fall off during baking).

7. Using a sharp knife, cut the dough into ⅛-inch slices and place on a baking sheet, spacing about 1 inch apart.

8. Bake for 12-15 minutes until crisp. Transfer to a cooling rack to cool completely.

9. Cookies can be stored in an airtight container at room temperature for up to 1 week.

MAKES **90** COOKIES

Palmiers (Elephant Ears)

Made from puff pastry
in the shape of a palm or butterfly,
palmiers are easy-to-prepare
French pastries that your
whole family will enjoy.

Ingredients

1 cup sugar
¼ cup cinnamon
1 tablespoon lemon zest
14 oz. frozen puff pastry, thawed
½ stick (2 oz.) butter, melted

Preparation

1. In a medium bowl, mix together the sugar, cinnamon and lemon zest. Working on a well-floured surface, roll out the puff pastry dough to a 10-inch x 6-inch rectangle, ⅛-inch thick. Brush the dough with the melted butter and sprinkle on the sugar mixture evenly.

2. Preheat oven to 400°F. Roll up one side of the dough along the edges lengthwise to the center (halfway); repeat with the other side. Using a sharp knife, cut the dough into slices, ½-inch thick.

3. Transfer cookies to a baking sheet, spacing about 1 inch apart. Bake for 20-22 minutes until golden and crisp. Transfer to a cooling rack to cool completely.

4. Cookies can be stored in an airtight container at room temperature for up 3 days.

MAKES 50 COOKIES

Baklava

MAKES **40** COOKIES

Baklava is a very sweet, rich cookie pastry made from phyllo dough and filled with chopped nuts. Historians believe that it has its origins in Ottoman Empire, while its current form was developed in the imperial kitchens of the Topkapi Palace in what is now geographically known as Turkey.

Ingredients

1¼ cups whole blanched almonds

7 oz. shelled pistachios

9.5 oz. walnuts

2 cups sugar

½ cup ground cinnamon

2½ sticks (10 oz.) butter, melted

½ cup canola oil

15 phyllo dough sheets

For syrup

1½ cups sugar

½ cup honey

2 cups water

Preparation

1. Place the almonds, pistachios, walnuts, sugar and cinnamon in a food processor and pulse until the mixture turns to crumbs. In a medium bowl, mix together the butter and canola oil. Preheat oven to 340°F.

2. *Assemble the baklava:* Place a sheet of phyllo dough on a baking sheet lined with parchment paper, and brush generously with the butter and oil mixture. Sprinkle a thin, even layer of the nut mixture. Repeat this process another 4 times, and then top with three sheets of phyllo, brushing in between each step.

3. Repeat another 5 times (dough, butter, nuts) and on the fifth layer place all of the remaining nut mixture (should be a thicker layer than the rest), and top with remaining two sheets of phyllo, brushing in between. Bake for 20 minutes until golden.

4. *Make the syrup:* Place sugar, honey and water in a medium saucepan on high heat and bring to a boil. Continue to cook for 5 minutes and remove from heat. Immediately upon removing the baklava from the oven, pour the syrup over it. Allow to chill completely. Using a sharp knife, cut out 3 triangles.

5. Cookies may be stored in an airtight container at room temperature for up to 1 week.

Langues-de-Chat (Lady Fingers)

These cookies get their name from their distinctive long, thin shape. They are great on their own, but even better when served with ice cream.

Ingredients

¾ stick (3 oz.) butter, at room temperature
1 cup powdered sugar
4 egg whites
1 teaspoon pure vanilla extract
1 cup all-purpose flour
½ cup sugar

Preparation

1. Using a mixer fitted with a whisk attachment, mix together the butter and powdered sugar on medium speed for 2 minutes, until light and creamy. Add the egg whites, one at a time, and then add the vanilla extract.

2. Reduce mixer speed to low and gradually add the flour. Continue mixing until all ingredients are combined.

3. Preheat oven to 350°F. Transfer batter to a pastry bag fitted with a round tip. Pipe 2-inch lengths, with ends slightly wider than the center, onto baking sheets lined with parchment paper, spacing about 1 inch apart. Sprinkle sugar evenly over cookies.

4. Bake for 8-10 minutes, until just golden around the edges. Transfer to a cooling rack to cool completely.

5. Cookies can be stored in an airtight container at room temperature for up 3 days.

MAKES 45 COOKIES

Classic Tuile

While warm, tuiles may be
molded into different shapes.
To make edible bowls for serving
mousse or ice cream, shape
the warm cookies over
upside-down cups.

Ingredients

¾ stick (3 oz.) butter, at room temperature
1 cup powdered sugar
4 egg whites
1 teaspoon pure vanilla extract
¾ cup all-purpose flour
¼ teaspoon salt

Preparation

1. Using a mixer fitted with a whisk attachment, mix together the butter and powdered sugar on medium speed for 2 minutes. Gradually add the egg whites, vanilla extract, flour and salt until all ingredients are combined well. Cover bowl in plastic wrap and refrigerate for 2 hours.

2. Preheat oven to 400°F. Drop 1 tablespoon of batter onto a silicon baking sheet spacing 2 inches apart. Use an offset spatula to flatten each to 5-inch rounds. Repeat with remaining batter.

3. Bake for 4-5 minutes until tuiles turn light gold in color. Remove from oven and quickly begin shaping them: use an offset spatula to remove cookies from sheet and immediately drape them over a rolling pin, on the bottom side of a cup, or over a wooden spoon handle, depending on desired shape. Let cookies cool slightly before removing. Allow to cool completely before serving.

4. Cookies can be stored in an airtight container at room temperature for up to 1 week.

MAKES 40 COOKIES

Biscotti

Also known as "Biscotti del Prato" or "Cantuccini", biscotti originate from the Italian city of Prato. These cookies are baked twice!

Ingredients

3 cups all-purpose flour

1¼ cups sugar

3 eggs

2 tablespoons Amaretto
(almond-flavored liqueur)

½ teaspoon salt

1 teaspoon baking powder

2 oz. whole blanched almonds

3 oz. raw, shelled pistachios

2 oz. walnuts

½ cup light raisins

Preparation

1. Using a mixer fitted with a dough hook, mix together the flour, sugar, eggs, Amaretto, salt, and baking powder on low speed for 2 minutes. Add the almonds, pistachios, walnuts and raisins and continue to mix until all ingredients are combined.

2. Working on a lightly floured surface, shape the dough into 12-inch x 3-inch logs. Flatten logs to 1½ inches thick. Wrap logs in plastic wrap and refrigerate for 1 hour.

3. Preheat oven to 300°F. Transfer logs to baking sheet lined with parchment paper and bake for 30-35 minutes, until golden. Allow to cool completely on a cooling rack before slicing. Once cool, cut each log along the diagonal into ⅛-inch slices.

4. Transfer slices to baking sheet lined with parchment paper and bake in oven for another 20 minutes at 280°F. Transfer to a cooling rack to cool completely before serving.

5. Cookies may be stored in an airtight container at room temperature for up to 2 weeks.

MAKES 40 COOKIES

Alfajores

These Argentinean cookies call for Dulce de Leche, the popular South American sweet spread. You can find store-bought Dulce de Leche in most supermarket chains and at specialty food stores.

Ingredients

1½ cups cornstarch
1½ cups all-purpose flour
1 teaspoon baking powder
¼ teaspoon salt
1¾ sticks (7 oz.) butter, at room temperature
1½ cups powdered sugar
2 egg yolks + 1 egg
1 tablespoon pure vanilla extract
1 cup store-bought Dulce de Leche
2 cups shredded coconut

Preparation

1. In a large bowl, sift together cornstarch, flour, baking powder and salt.

2. Using a mixer fitted with a whisk attachment, mix together the butter and powdered sugar on medium speed for 2 minutes. Add the egg yolks, egg and vanilla extract and continue mixing until all ingredients are combined.

3. Reduce mixer speed to low and gradually add dry ingredients. Continue mixing until dough forms. Wrap dough in plastic wrap and refrigerate for 1 hour.

4. Preheat oven to 350°F. Working on a lightly floured surface, roll out the dough to ⅛ inch thick. Using a 2-inch round cookie cutter, cut out cookies and place on a baking sheet, spacing one inch apart.

5. Bake for 8-10 minutes. Transfer to a cooling rack to cool completely.

6. *Make the cookie sandwich:* Spread 1 heaped teaspoon of Dulce de Leche over half of the cookies on their flat side; place a second cookie on top of the covered ones, creating sandwiches. Gently press the cookies together to spread the filling to the edges, and then smooth the edges with a small offset spatula or knife. Roll the cookies in the shredded coconut.

7. Cookie sandwiches can be stored in an airtight container at room temperature for up to 3 days.

MAKES 30 SANDWICHES

Roulade Date Cookies

I like to use Medjool dates for this recipe, as I find them the most flavorful and meatiest of all varieties.

Ingredients

1¾ sticks (7 oz.) butter, cubed

1½ cups all-purpose flour

¼ teaspoon salt

¾ cup ground almonds

¾ cup powdered sugar

1 egg

2 tablespoons milk

For filling

2¼ cups pitted dates

½ cup walnuts, coarsely chopped

2 tablespoons cinnamon

Preparation

1. Using a mixer fitted with a paddle attachment, mix together the butter, flour, salt, ground almonds and powdered sugar on medium speed for 2 minutes, until mixture has a crumb-like texture. Add the egg and milk and continue to mix until all ingredients are combined and dough forms.

2. Divide the dough into two equal parts, wrap in plastic wrap and refrigerate for 1 hour.

3. ***Make the filling:*** Place dates in a medium saucepan and cover with water. Bring to a boil on medium heat. Reduce heat and simmer for about 15 minutes, until dates are soft and liquid has reduced. Remove from heat and let cool completely. Transfer dates to a food processor and puree until mixture is smooth.

4. Preheat oven to 340°F. Working on a lightly floured surface, roll out one dough ball to a 14-inch x 10-inch rectangle, ⅛-inch thick. Using an offset spatula or flat flexible spatula, spread a thin layer of the date puree onto the dough. Sprinkle half of the chopped walnuts and cinnamon evenly over the puree. Roll up one side of the dough along the edges lengthwise, and place log onto a baking sheet lined with parchment paper. Repeat with second dough ball.

5. Bake for 22-25 minutes until golden. Transfer to a cooling rack to cool completely. Using a serrated knife, cut the log into slices, ½-inch thick.

6. Decorate with powdered sugar and serve.

7. Cookies can be stored in an airtight container at room temperature for up 3 days.

MAKES **40** COOKIES

Orange Ginger Cookies

MAKES **50** COOKIES

You can find candied ginger at any supermarket, or get creative and make your own homemade candied ginger using fresh ginger, sugar, water and salt.

Ingredients

2 sticks (8 oz.) butter, at room temperature

1 cup powdered sugar

½ teaspoon orange zest

2 egg yolks

2½ cups all-purpose flour, sifted

1 tablespoon ground cardamom

¼ teaspoon salt

2.5 oz. ground almonds

3.5 oz. candied ginger, cut into ¼-inch pieces

For royal icing

1 egg white

2¼ cups powdered sugar

1 tablespoon orange liqueur
(such as Grand Marnier) or orange juice

2-3 drops of natural orange food coloring

Preparation

1. Using a stand mixer fitted with a paddle attachment, mix the butter, powdered sugar and orange zest on medium speed for 2-3 minutes until combined well. Add the egg yolks and mix for 1 minute.

2. In a large bowl, sift together the flour, ground almonds, salt and cardamom.

3. Gradually add the dry ingredients to the mixer, and then add the candied ginger. Mix for another 2 minutes until all ingredients are combined.

4. Roll out the dough to about ⅛-inch thick, place onto a baking sheet and refrigerate for at least 3 hours.

5. *Make the royal icing:* In a large bowl, whisk the egg white, gradually add the powdered sugar, and mix until the mixture is the consistency of a paste. Add the orange liqueur/orange juice and the food coloring, until the desired color is reached.

6. Remove the dough from the refrigerator. Using a spatula, spread a ⅛ inch layer of icing over the dough.

7. Using a sharp knife, cut the dough into 1½-inch cubes (you should clean your knife after every cut). Set aside at room temperature for about 1 hour until the icing hardens.

8. Bake in a preheated oven at 350°F for 12-15 minutes. Transfer to a cooling rack to cool completely.

9. Cookies may be stored in an airtight container at room temperature for up to 1 week.

marmalade

Marmalade Squares

A baking thermometer is crucial to the success of these marmalade squares. You can find it at any specialized baking shop.

Ingredients

3⅓ cups fresh fruit juice (passion fruit, berry, orange, or grapefruit), strained

2½ tablespoons pectin

½ cup sugar + 4½ cups sugar

⅔ cup glucose or light corn syrup

1 teaspoon cream of tartar

For coating

1 cup sugar

For baking

One 6½- inch square metal ring, lined with a silicon baking sheet or parchment paper

Sugar (candy) thermometer

Preparation

1. In a large saucepan, heat the fruit juice to 104°F. Add the pectin and ½ cup of sugar and stir continuously until just barely simmering.

2. Add the 4½ cups of sugar and corn syrup and continue to stir until the mixture reaches exactly 228°F.

3. Then add the cream of tartar and mix. Immediately remove mixture from heat and pour it evenly into the square metal ring.

4. Let the mixture cool to room temperature. Once completely cool, use a sharp knife to cut out 1-inch squares and coat each square with sugar.

5. Cookies can be stored in the airtight container at room temperature for up to 2 weeks.

MAKES **40** SQUARES

Banana & Hazelnut Cookies

These moist, rich cookies are the perfect combination of cookie and cake; banana and hazelnut.

Ingredients

2 cups all-purpose flour

¼ teaspoon salt

½ teaspoon baking powder

¼ teaspoon baking soda

2 sticks (8 oz.) butter, at room temperature

1 cup sugar

1 tablespoon pure vanilla extract

2 ripe bananas, mashed

2 eggs

1⅔ cups hazelnuts, coarsely chopped

Preparation

1. In a large bowl, sift together the flour, salt, baking powder and baking soda.

2. Using a mixer fitted with paddle attachment, mix together the butter, sugar, vanilla extract and bananas on medium speed for 3 minutes, until creamy. Add the eggs, one at a time, and continue mixing until combined. Reduce mixer speed to low and gradually add the dry ingredients.

3. Continue to mix for another 2 minutes, until all ingredients are combined and dough forms. Add the hazelnuts and mix for 1 minute. Wrap dough in plastic wrap and refrigerate for 2 hours.

4. Preheat oven to 350°F. Using a 1½-inch ice cream scoop, drop dough onto baking sheets lined with parchment paper, spacing about 2 inches apart. Gently press each cookie to flatten slightly.

5. Bake for 18-20 minutes until golden. Transfer to a cooling rack to cool completely.

6. Cookies may be stored in an airtight container at room temperature for up to 1 week.

MAKES **35** COOKIES

Marzipan

Though Marzipan is believed
to have originated in Persia
and been introduced to Europe
through the Turks,
both Hungary and Italy also claim
to have a stake in its conception.

Ingredients

⅓ cup water
1 teaspoon lemon juice
1 cup sugar
½ cup ground almonds
15 whole shelled pistachios
For baking
Baking thermometer

Preparation

1. In a small saucepan, cook the water, lemon juice and sugar on low heat until the mixture reaches 250°F (using a baking thermometer) and the mixture turns to syrup.

2. Reduce heat, add the ground almonds, and stir continuously for 2 minutes on low heat, until the mixture thickens.

3. Remove from heat and transfer mixture to a work surface lined with parchment paper to cool for 5 minutes. When the mixture is still warm, transfer to a food processor and blend for 3 minutes, until the mixture has a crumb-like consistency.

4. Remove mixture from food processor and knead the mixture until it forms a ball.

5. Remove pieces from the ball to form 1-inch balls. Firmly press one pistachio into each ball.

6. Cookies may be stored in an airtight container in the refrigerator for up to 1 week.

MAKES **15** COOKIES

Scottish Shortbread

The story of Scottish shortbread begins with the medieval "biscuit bread". Leftover dough from the bread-making was dried out in a low oven until it hardened. Gradually, the yeast in the bread was replaced by butter and the biscuit bread developed into Scottish shortbread.

Ingredients

2½ cups all-purpose flour
¼ teaspoon salt
2 sticks (8 oz.) butter, at room temperature
½ cup sugar
2 tablespoons pure vanilla extract
For decoration
½ cup powdered sugar
For baking
One 8-inch square baking dish

Preparation

1. In a medium bowl, sift together the flour and salt.

2. Using a mixer fitted with a whisk attachment, mix together the butter, sugar and vanilla extract on medium speed for 3 minutes, until fluffy.

3. Reduce mixer speed to low. Gradually add the flour mixture and mix just until all ingredients are combined. Do not over mix.

4. Preheat oven to 300°F. Transfer dough to an 8-inch square baking dish lined with parchment paper, spreading evenly until the dough is ¾-inch thick. Using a fork, prick all over at ¼-inch intervals.

5. Bake for 50-55 minutes until just barely golden. When still hot, use a sharp knife to cut 1-inch squares. Allow to cool completely on a wire rack. Decorate with powdered sugar and serve.

6. Cookies can be stored in an airtight container at room temperature for up to 1 week.

MAKES 45 COOKIES

Conversion Charts

USEFUL EQUIVALENTS FOR COOKING/OVEN TEMPERATURES

	Fahrenheit	Celsius	Gas Mark
Freeze Water	32° F	0° C	
Room Temp.	68° F	20° C	
Boil Water	212° F	100° C	
Bake	325° F	160° C	3
	350° F	180° C	4
	375° F	190° C	5
	400° F	200° C	6
	425° F	220° C	7
	450° F	230° C	8
Broil			Grill

USEFUL EQUIVALENTS FOR LIQUID INGREDIENTS BY VOLUME

				1 ml	
¼ tsp				2 ml	
½ tsp				5 ml	
1 tsp	1 tbls		½ fl oz	15 ml	
3 tsp	2 tbls	⅛ cup	1 fl oz	30 ml	
	4 tbls	¼ cup	2 fl oz	60 ml	
	5⅓ tbls	⅓ cup	3 fl oz	80 ml	
	8 tbls	½ cup	4 fl oz	120 ml	
	10⅔ tbls	⅔ cup	5 fl oz	160 ml	
	12 tbls	¾ cup	6 fl oz	180 ml	
	16 tbls	1 cup	8 fl oz	240 ml	
	1 pt	2 cups	16 fl oz	480 ml	
	1 qt	4 cups	32 fl oz	960 ml	
			33 fl oz	1000 ml	1 liter

The recipes that appear in this cookbook use the standard United States method for measuring liquid and dry or solid ingredients (teaspoons, tablespoons, and cups). The information on this chart is provided to help cooks outside the U.S. successfully use these recipes. All equivalents are approximate.

METRIC EQUIVALENTS FOR DIFFERENT TYPES OF INGREDIENTS

A standard cup measure of a dry or solid ingredient will vary in weight depending on the type of ingredient. A standard cup of liquid is the same volume for any type of liquid. Use the following chart when converting standard cup measures to grams (weight) or milliliters (volume).

Standard Cup	Fine Powder *(ex. flour)*	Grain *(ex.rice)*	Granular *(ex. sugar)*	Liquid Solids *(ex. butter)*	Liquid *(ex. milk)*
1	140 g	150 g	190 g	200 g	240 ml
¾	105 g	113 g	143 g	150 g	180 ml
⅔	93 g	100 g	125 g	133 g	160 ml
½	70 g	75 g	95 g	100 g	120 ml
⅓	47 g	50 g	63 g	67 g	80 ml
¼	35 g	38 g	48 g	50 g	60 ml
¼	18 g	19 g	24 g	25 g	30 ml

USEFUL EQUIVALENTS FOR DRY INGREDIENTS BY WEIGHT

To convert ounces	1 oz.	1⁄16 lb	30g
to grams, multiply	4 oz.	¼ lb	120g
the number of	8 oz.	½ lb	240g
ounces by 30.	12 oz.	1 lb	480g

USEFUL EQUIVALENTS FOR LENGTH

To convert inches	1 in			2.5 cm	
to centimeters	6 in			15 cm	
multiply number of	12 in	½ ft		30 cm	
inches by 2.5.	36 in	1 ft		90 cm	
	40 in	3 ft	1 yd	100 cm	1 m

Index